To Paul —
with appreciation
and respect —
Brigitte + Howard

MW01712708

Integral House

The 2006 Martell Lecture

Published to celebrate the annual Martell Lecture given by Brigitte Shim on March 31, 2006 at the School of Architecture and Planning, University at Buffalo, The State University of New York.

Editor: Annette LeCuyer
Design: Christian Unverzagt with Neil Meredith at M1/DTW
Typeset in Avenir
Printed and bound in the United States of America

ISBN 10: 0-9771057-3-3
ISBN 13: 978-0-9771057-3-1

© 2006 School of Architecture and Planning,
University at Buffalo, The State University of New York

School of Architecture and Planning
Hayes Hall
3435 Main Street
Buffalo, NY 14214-3087

716 829 3485
716 829 2297 fax
www.ap.buffalo.edu

Integral House

Shim·Sutcliffe

The 2006 Martell Lecture

Established in 1969, the School of Architecture and Planning at the University at Buffalo is relatively young. However, many of our 3,722 alumni provide invaluable support. Through the generosity of Christopher Martell, an alumnus of both the undergraduate and graduate architecture programs at UB, and his wife Sally, we have been able to launch a new initiative in the School.

The appointment of the Martell Distinguished Visiting Critic is an annual event that is already a significant landmark in our academic year. It brings an internationally renowned architect to Buffalo and The State University of New York's only accredited architecture program. This guest works with a group of graduate students in the design studio during the semester and gives a public lecture. In order to share the ideas from that lecture with as wide an audience as possible, the Martells also support a publication that is distributed through a network of global bookshops, university libraries, colleagues in academia and the profession, students and alumni. Steven Holl was the first Martell Distinguished Visiting Critic in 2005.

Christopher and Sally Martell are enthusiastic supporters of UB. They are interested in design, keen to advance a program that brings new and inspiring ideas about architecture to our School and committed to projecting those ideas widely. We are grateful for their continued generosity, which makes it possible to build quality, diversity and accessibility in our program. The appointment of the outstanding Canadian architect Brigitte Shim as the 2006 Martell Distinguished Visiting Critic highlights our mutual and continuing interest in focusing on excellence in architecture and planning in Buffalo.

Brian Carter
Professor and Dean
The School of Architecture and Planning
University at Buffalo, The State University of New York

Introduction

To say that Brigitte Shim and Howard Sutcliffe are interested in materials would be banal and generic, as of course every architect is interested in materials. That is what buildings are made of: good ones, as well as bad ones; old ones, as well as new ones. To say that they are interested in wood, water and weathering steel, as they have, seems as generic as the first on a cursory read, yet contains clues to a more particular and decisive interest in materials. Water is an element of nature, wood an element of nature that is controlled and shaped, and weathering steel, a manufactured material that is designed to conspire with and react to the forces of nature.

In the selection and listing of these materials, Shim and Sutcliffe have given us a particular lens through which we can see their work. This is not a lens that highlights these three materials, but one that illuminates an interest in provoking an intense relationship between the natural and the man-made, between a precision break-formed piece of steel and its unpredictable weathering, between the natural grain of a piece of wood and its unnaturally red-dyed color.

This calculated provocation of intensity between the wild and unpredictable forces of nature and the controlled processes of contemporary fabrication has marked the work of Shim·Sutcliffe, at once universal and singular; at once global and local. At once as particular as the vast post-glacial Canadian landscape and as universal as that place where Brigitte Shim and Howard Sutcliffe live and work – a place that covers ten percent of the globe, from longitude 0 to 125 West of Greenwich, and from latitude 17 to 60, from temperate to arctic, from volcanic to glacial.

Mehrdad Hadighi
Chair of Architecture

It is an honor to be the Martell Distinguished Visiting Critic at the University at Buffalo. It has been a particular pleasure to spend time in the school and to work with students in the studio throughout this semester.

Howard and I have built our studio in Toronto around teaching and practice. It is a small studio, and a significant part of our work there has focused on the design of modest projects that include landscape and furniture, public spaces and private houses. The modern house, which transformed understandings of space and site, played a powerful role in the development of architecture in the twentieth century. Canonical modern buildings – like Rietveld's Schroeder-Schrader House, the Farnsworth House by Ludwig Mies van der Rohe and the Villa Savoye by Le Corbusier; or Aalto's Villa Mairea, the Maison de Verre by Pierre Chareau, and Buffalo's Darwin Martin House designed by Frank Lloyd Wright – have each expanded and redefined the possibilities of architecture. They are not large projects but, through their domestic scale, have been an important laboratory for experimentation and the exploration of new ideas in design.

When I go to see a movie, I inevitably sit through the credits and am always surprised by the number of people it takes to make a film. When you design and build a building, you realize that anything that challenges the status quo requires a similarly long list of collaborators. Because of its unusual scope, the design and construction of the Integral House are the result of many people's talents and commitments. Our client, Dr. James Stewart, is a mathematician and teacher who writes calculus textbooks. He is also a musician and has a keen interest in architecture and design. Working together with Professor Larry Richards, former Dean of the Faculty of Architecture, Landscape and Design at the University of Toronto, they prepared a brief that eloquently described his requirements, sensibilities and architectural aspirations for the project. After visiting numerous houses and the studios of many architects including Frank Gehry and Steven Holl, we were selected to design a house for Jim Stewart. It was to be a place to live and work, and which would also become the venue for musical and theatrical performances. The project is an exploration of ideas about space, volume and light that revolve around our client's needs and grow out of the qualities of a remarkable sloping site overlooking a ravine in Toronto. The house will be completed in the fall of 2007.

All of our built work to date has been in Canada. However, this should not be misunderstood as a single context. We have worked in many specific and distinctly different settings, ranging from distant sites in the north of the province to urban conditions in the center of Toronto. We have learned that the culture of building varies widely from place to place and not always in the ways anticipated. On a number of the remote sites, the range of labor skills and high levels of craftsmanship have surprised us. Consequently, wherever we are working, we start by learning about the local construction culture and seeking out the best craftsmen in the area. The contractors who are building the Integral House, together with the many consultants, are people we have worked with on a number of projects.

Over the years, we have built up shared design and construction experience as well as a common understanding of what is important at each stage of the project. The contractors were retained early in the process to review both preliminary drawings and models and later, more developed construction details. This allowed them to play an important role in the evolution of the project, with their input incorporated into the final drawings and specifications. As an alternative to the more adversarial relationship that characterizes many North American construction sites, this process has focused on working as a team. This project has definitely been a challenge, and the transformation of idea to building has been realized only with the collaboration of this group of designers, builders and fabricators.

The intensity and breadth of detail of the Integral House were developed through conversations, sketches, drawings, models and the construction and testing of numerous full size mock-ups. They highlight some of the aspects that, for us, are most significant in understanding the essence of the idea of this building and its evolution into three dimensional form. This book is not about a finished building represented by carefully composed and edited images, but rather an attempt to unravel a building's evolution. By describing and revealing a process that documents the scheme from initial sketches through to working drawings, we hope to demonstrate that design does not happen magically.

Although the Integral House has engaged us in the exploration of new territory, several of our previous projects provide a context for the understanding of this scheme. Our first commission, a tiny garden pavilion at the edge of a ravine in Toronto, was completed in 1989. It was an early manifesto that explored the relationship between landscape, building, architecture and furniture, and we have developed these themes subsequently in a range of projects. When we think about our work, we try to imagine what it will look like over time, what it will look like when it is overgrown, in contrast with the moment of its completion, which is always within a landscape that has yet to mature. Recent photos of this project show its lush condition after seventeen years – one that we would like to think was in our mind's eye at the time the pavilion was designed.

The scheme engages the ravine through sectional development and explores the use of water. The garden pavilion was an early experiment that laid the groundwork for fundamental concerns in our current work. It foreshadowed aspects of the Integral House, which is a more elaborate version of the idea of descending into a landscape and a space at the same time, and of making the experience of the changing seasons part of daily life.

The Ravine Guest House, built on the same site for the same client, was completed in 2005. Here again, water and the landscape interlock with built form. The fireplace is a figural, free-standing object in a single room that frames views of the landscape.

Good buildings need good friends. Much of our work at Massey College at the University of Toronto, a significant building designed by Ron Thom and completed in 1963, has been to provide a level of stewardship to accommodate new needs and to do this in a way that understands the original intent.
Our interventions add a layer to the building without mimicking what exists. A new lining of weathering steel in the entryway provides a sitting area that works with the existing brick walls, and we have designed a new west gate and much-needed log storage for the original fireplaces which the architect planned in every room. We have also reconfigured the college's Robertson Davies Library. As a junior fellow at Massey College, Jim Stewart spent many hours in this library and in the college common room, which is a living room for the students and faculty of the college as well as a place for hosting major events including lectures, recitals and socials. These experiences brought an understanding that such special occasions, celebrations and day-to-day living are not incompatible and, significantly for the brief of the Integral House, prompted the simultaneous consideration of grand and intimate spaces.

In contrast with our projects in Toronto, a house on one of the Thousand Islands in the St. Lawrence Seaway is sited in a gently rolling and open landscape. Approached from a small country road, the front elevation, tucked below a green roof, is private and enigmatic. The view and the volume of space are not evident when you walk in the door but open up as you descend within. Upon entering, you are in the upper third of the living space, which is enclosed by a translucent fiberglass

wall. You then descend a few feet to the living area, which is surrounded by a reflecting pool that is almost as large as the house itself. As the cubic volume of the living room unfolds, you are aware of the wrapping of the reflecting pool and of the living room volume emerging out of something that appeared at first to be very horizontal. This volume reads in quite different ways. From the outside, the fiberglass upper portion floats above the clear glass and a landscape of natural grasses. At night, it is like a paper lantern in the meadow. We wanted to capture these same qualities in the Integral House.

In the Corkin Shopland Gallery in the Distillery District of Toronto, the found condition was a series of brick walls five feet on center that were originally the supports for huge vats of pure spirits. Arched openings in the walls enabled workmen to move across the space below the vats. These industrial buildings, used for 140 years, were eventually abandoned and are now finally being brought back into use as a new cultural district in the city. This gallery for contemporary art has been designed as an insertion into the walls that define the space. Two new gallery volumes flank a double height carved out exhibition area in the center of the space. The route once used for workers to service the vats becomes part of a circulation system that connects the exhibition areas to the gallery library on a new glazed bridge floating above the brick piers. Unlike the Integral House, which focuses external views, this is an internal landscape that explores light through translucent planes and layered space.

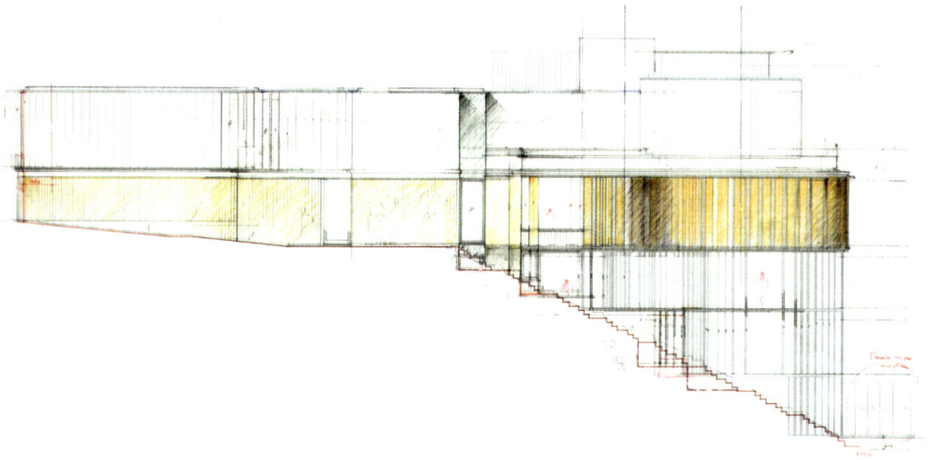

The integral symbol is the function symbol of calculus. It also refers to the discrete elements of this house being part of a greater whole. This symbol is not only a reference to the life of the mathematician client, but finds itself in the curves of the house and in the types of geometry used in the wall systems. The Integral House sits at the edge of a Toronto ravine. From the street, it appears as a two story structure with a translucent glass pavilion floating above a more grounded wooden base. As the solid wall of the base curves out to enclose the living areas, it dissolves into a series of fins. The glass wall above and the fin wall below meet at the entry to the house, where a large clear glass vestibule frames views through the house and forms a transition between the solid and more rectilinear service spaces and the porous, more fluid forms of the living spaces beyond.

The sectional experience is the key to understanding the house. Both the flat tableland and sloped ravine are legible in the floor plates, landings and stairs that form the architectural elements of the house. Although the previous house on the site was built in the ravine, current regulations allow construction only on the tableland. However, because of this previous house, the Integral House can occupy a unique position in the ravine. What appears to be a two story volume on the street is actually five stories as it reaches down the slope. The orthogonal portion of the house is on the tableland and the organic part of the house is in the ravine. The distinction between these two realms is important. On the tableland, the house is part of the city but as it descends, it leaves the city to become part of forest.

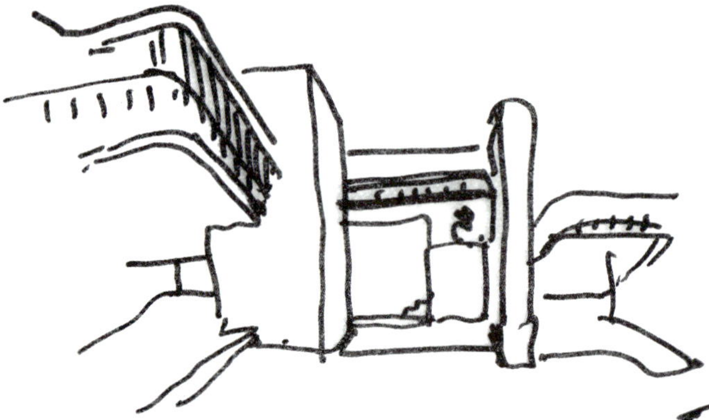

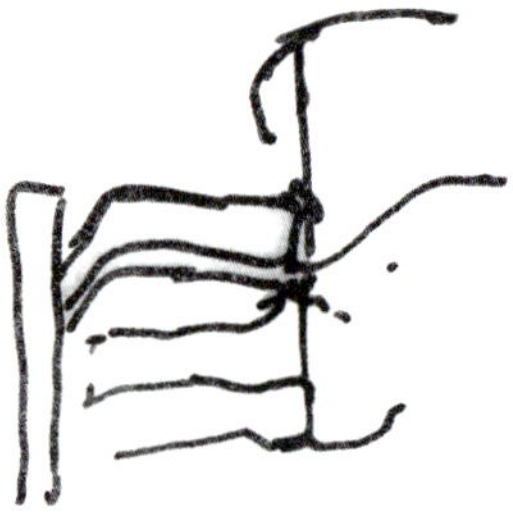

Upon entering the house, you step into the main living space, which doubles as a performance space. At this level, you are between the city and the forest – a suspended place floating amidst the trees. As you move into the performance area, the ceiling of the entry level pulls up to create a clerestory window while the floor drops away to reveal a double height volume overlooking the valley below. The kitchen, dining space and a small living area at the entry level overlook the double height living and performance space. Bedrooms are above on the top floor, while the level beneath the performance space houses a study and guest bedroom with a pool below.

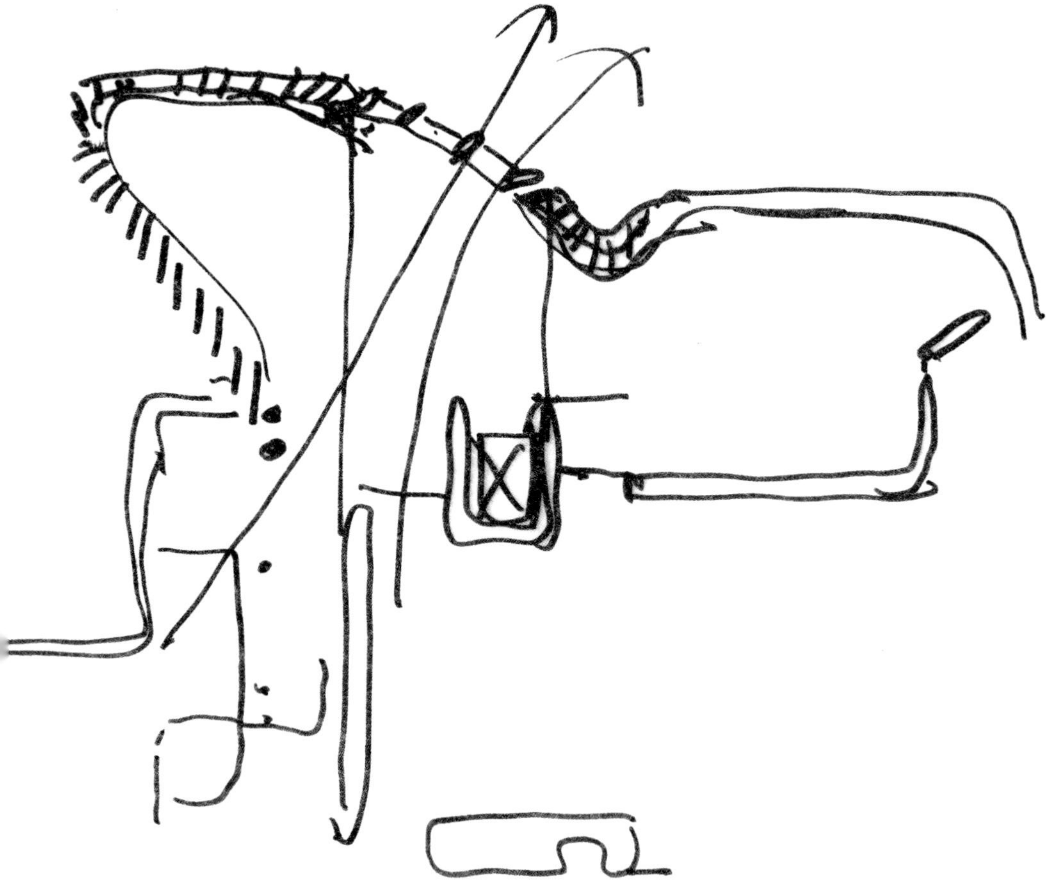

Within the undulating space, three free-standing vertical concrete elements – a chimney, an elevator shaft and a stairwell – anchor the space within the open plan and continuously recalibrate relationships to the interior spaces and to nature. They extend through all levels of the house from the pool to the upper bedrooms and serve as backdrops for three 'performance' pieces: a grand entry stair, a large hearth and an art glass wall. The chimney and elevator shaft frame steps from the entrance to create a switchback path that descends down the hillside to the performance space.

The section of the house parallels the experience of descending into the ravine and ascending to the tree tops. Each of the five floors has a different and emphatic relationship to the ground and the forest. At the lowest level, where the forest floor is primary, dark stone and moss emerge from the earth. Moving up, both the material palette and the spatial experience become lighter until they reach the bedrooms on the top floor, which are conceived as treehouse-like spaces. The house unfolds; you are unaware of the total volume until you move through it.

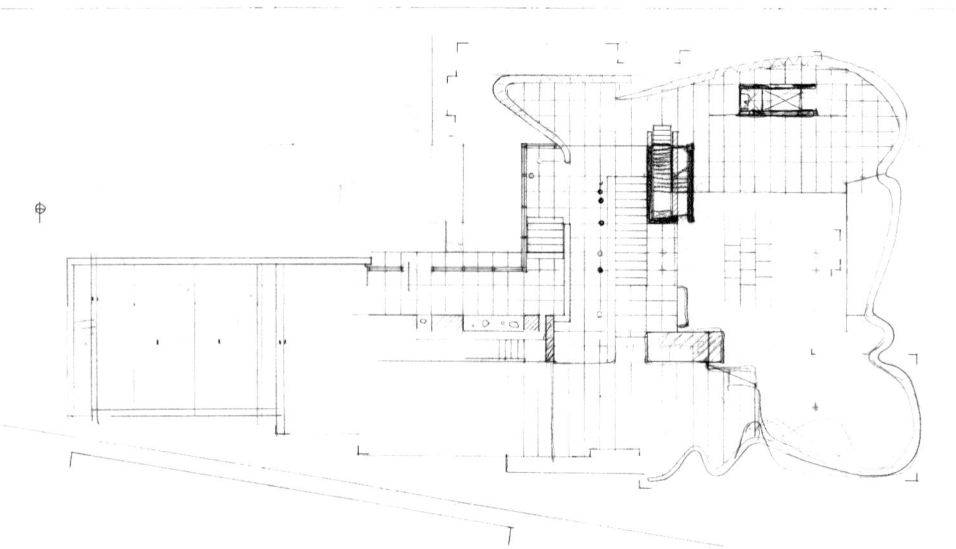

The plan developed gradually through a series of iterations. Sitting at a desk in studio, you might think this happens instantly. The truth is that it involves reworking the same thing over and over and over again to shape the final built form. In the early stages it is more amorphous, then with each reworking, it comes slowly into focus. However, even the earliest freehand perspectives and small study models contain the seeds of the distinctive feature of the house – an undulating glazed façade enclosing the generous two story performance space that hovers within the ravine. In contrast with the spatial experience, the undulating wall is dense above and permeable below. As you move down through the house into the ravine, it becomes more open.

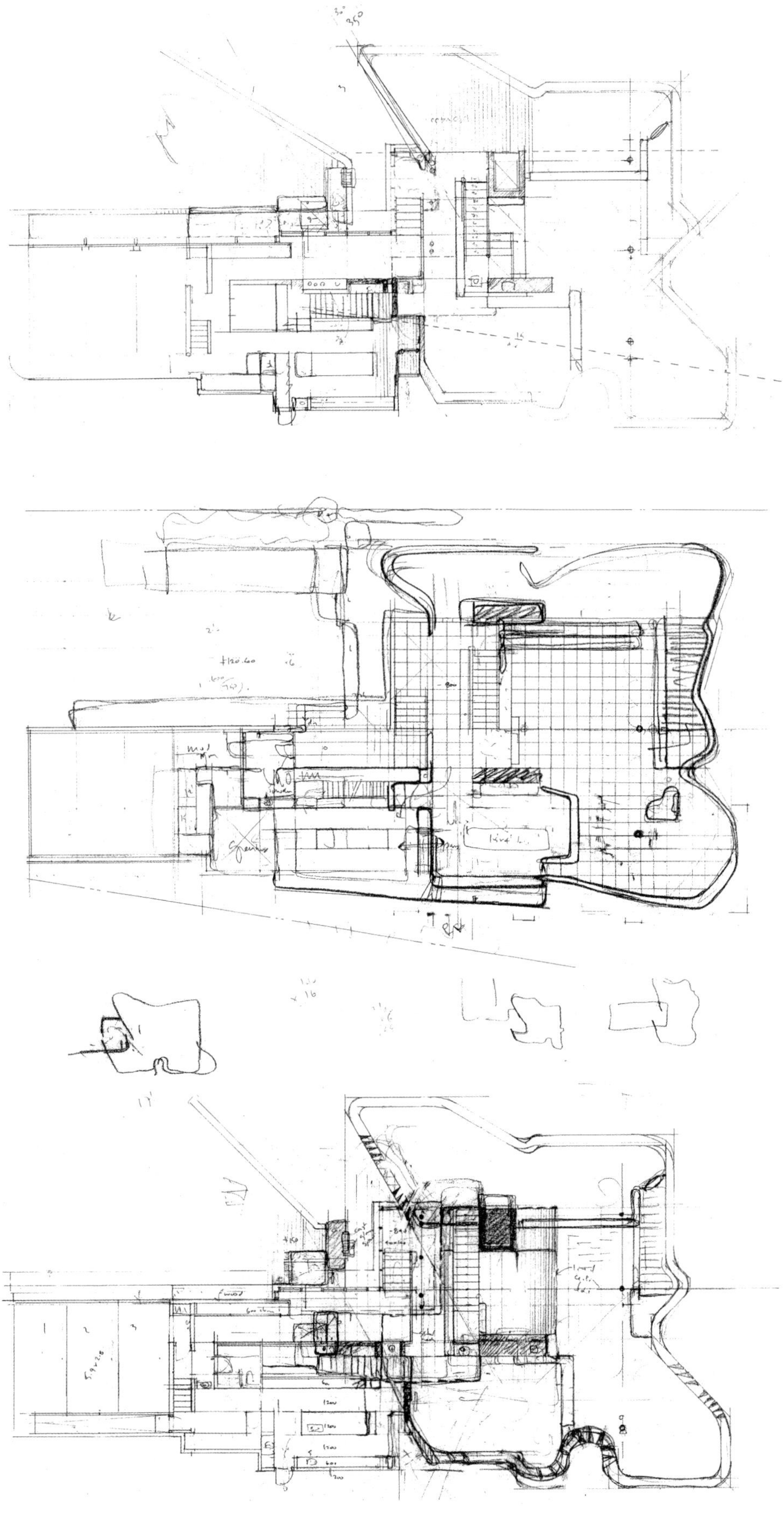

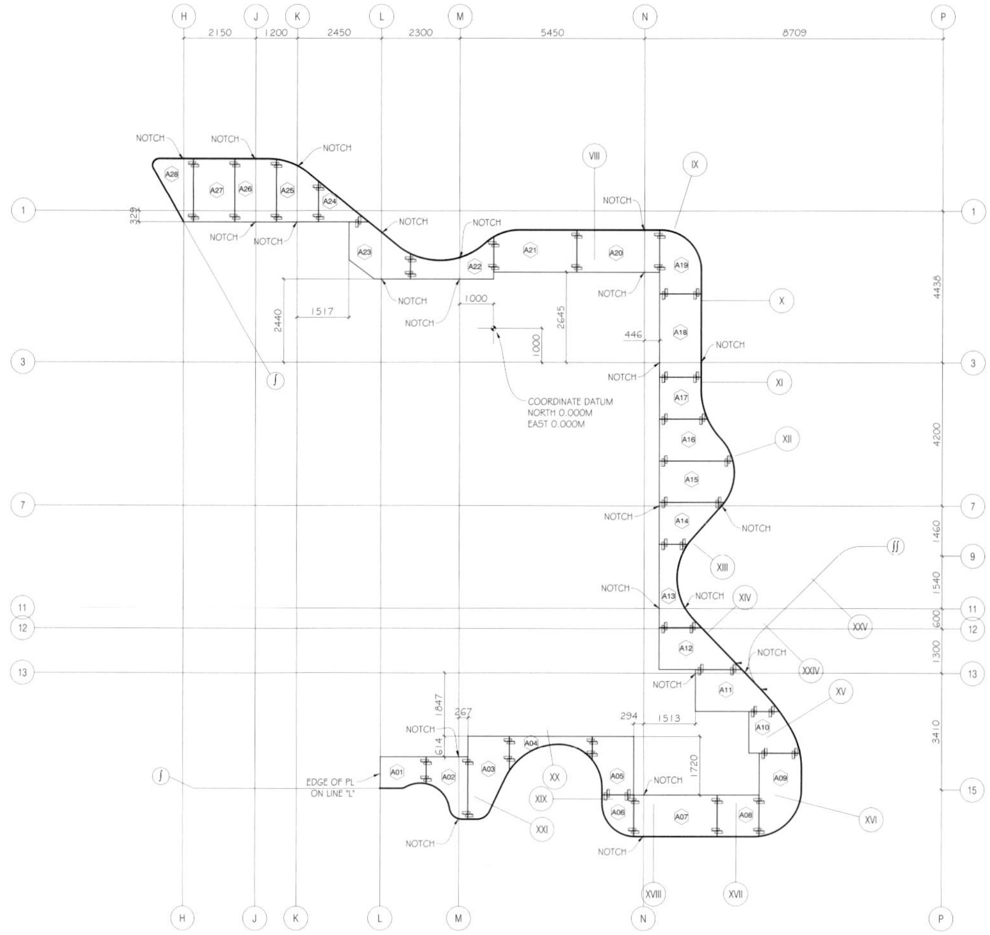

Early studies using both drawings and models focused our efforts on understanding the quality of light which passes through the undulating wall. It is comprised of a series of oak-clad fins arrayed in a syncopated rhythm that define the curving column line at the perimeter of the plan. We started calling the line we used to mark and build the curve the *summa* line because we had used alpha numeric symbols for the grids oriented in the cardinal directions and wanted another symbol for the curve. We used the integral symbol, which is also called the *sum* or *summa* symbol. Perhaps appropriately for this project, the word *summa* also means comprehensive treatise.

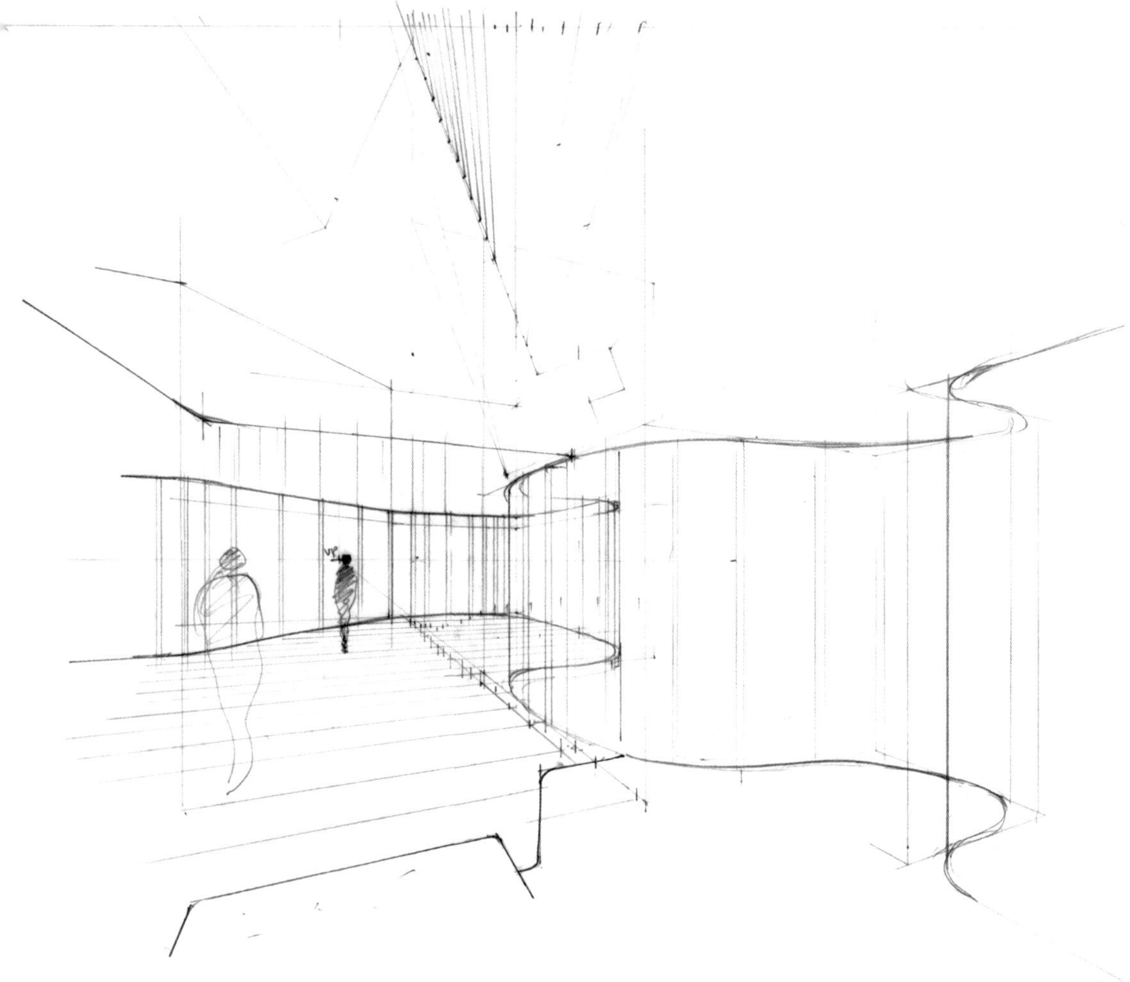

The folded, inside/outside spaces of the Integral House began to emerge in an earlier project. The house on Hurricane Lake in Haliburton has a double height outdoor space framed by the living room on one side and the bedrooms on the other, and crossed by a bridge. The continuous interlocking of inside and outside space with water, both designed and natural, is a key experience of the Haliburton house. Like many of our projects, the house reads at varying scales. When viewed from the forest, it is quite miniature and when viewed from the lake, it is more heroic.

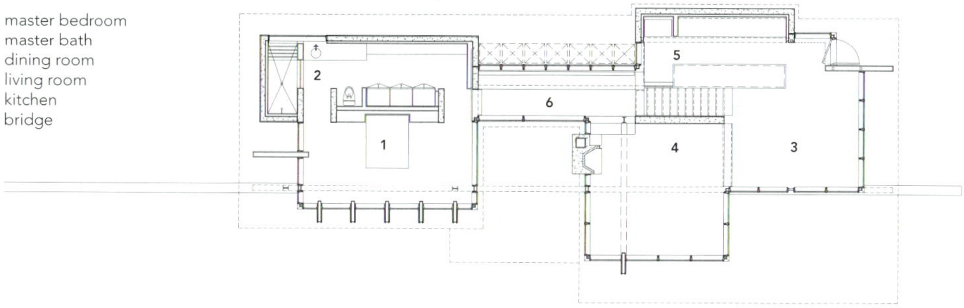

1 master bedroom
2 master bath
3 dining room
4 living room
5 kitchen
6 bridge

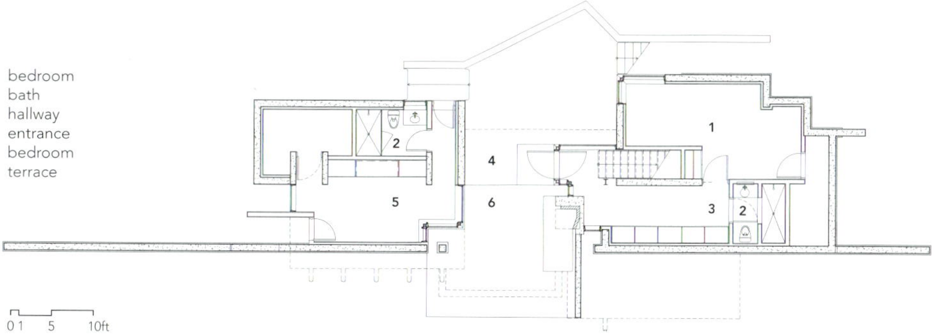

1 bedroom
2 bath
3 hallway
4 entrance
5 bedroom
6 terrace

While we have been interested in the relationship of architecture and landscape from our first project, the new aspect of the Integral House is this interweaving of building and landscape in the thick screen wall, so that views are constantly reframed as you move through the house. The relationship to the trees of the forest is direct and varying. Likewise, the changing shapes and orientations of the vertical fins seek to establish a dual relationship – between the occupant and nature, and the occupant and time. Movement through the house, like the passage of the sun and the seasons, changes both the quality and the perception of space. At times the perimeter fin wall appears to be solid, while a slight change of orientation opens the view to the ravine beyond. The dramatic curvature of the plan creates folded courtyard-like spaces. One sees outside, then back into the house beyond, to experience views that filter through the trees and the exterior façade, and layer both space and structure. It is an ensemble that attempts to weave together forest, building, people and movement. The fins simultaneously provide a vertical rhythm and two kinds of framing. At each window, one's relationship to the site is vertical, classical and individual. At the scale of an entire elevation, it is horizontal, panoramic and cinematic.

LEVEL 5

1 hall
2 powder room
3 elevator
4 master bath
5 master bedroom
6 roof terrace
7 media room
8 guest bathroom
9 guest room
10 guest suite

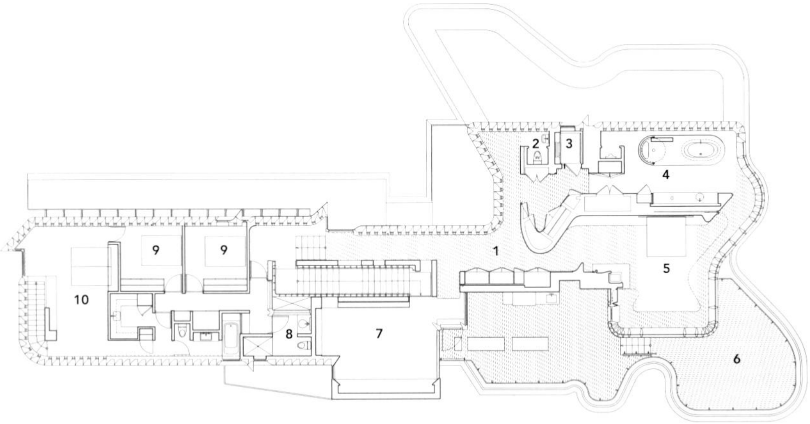

LEVEL 4

1 entry
2 reflecting pool
3 upper living room
4 dining room
5 kitchen
6 pantry
7 garage
8 elevator

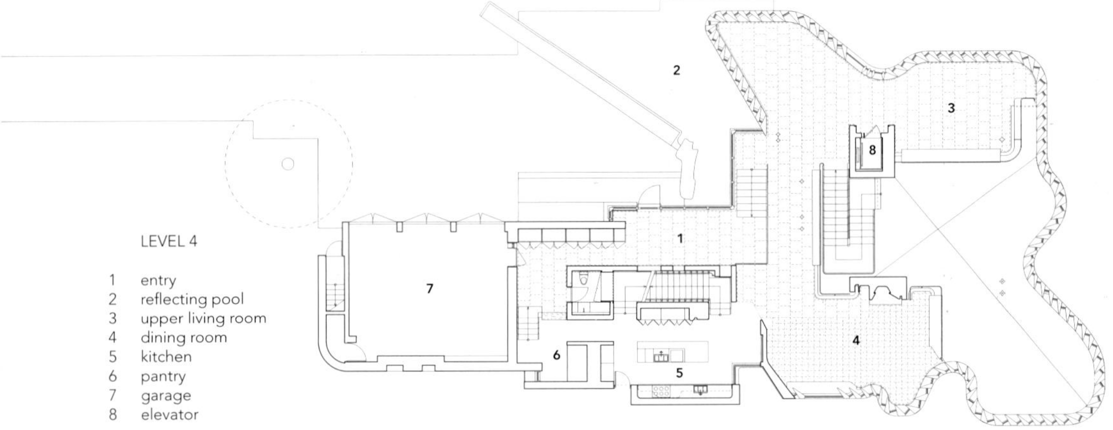

LEVEL 3

1 living room
2 family room
3 vestibule
4 bar
5 servery
6 storage
7 mechanical room
8 laundry
9 washroom
10 elevator

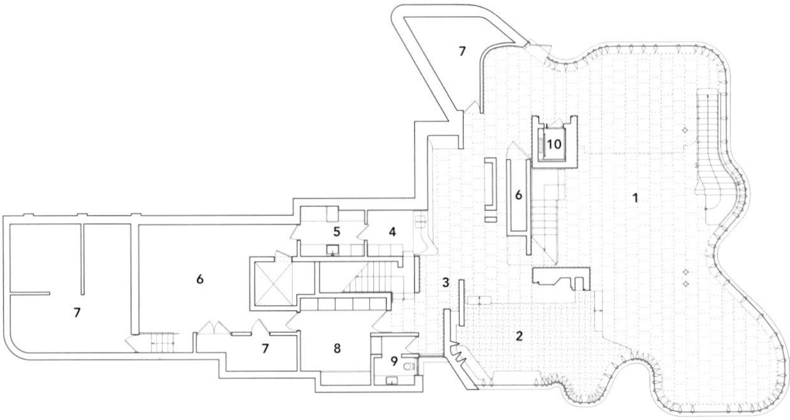

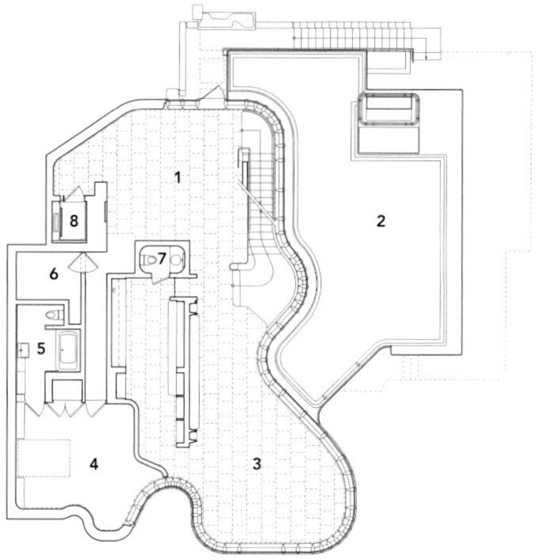

LEVEL 2

1 gallery
2 roof garden
3 study
4 guest bedroom
5 guest bath
6 mechanical room
7 washroom
8 elevator

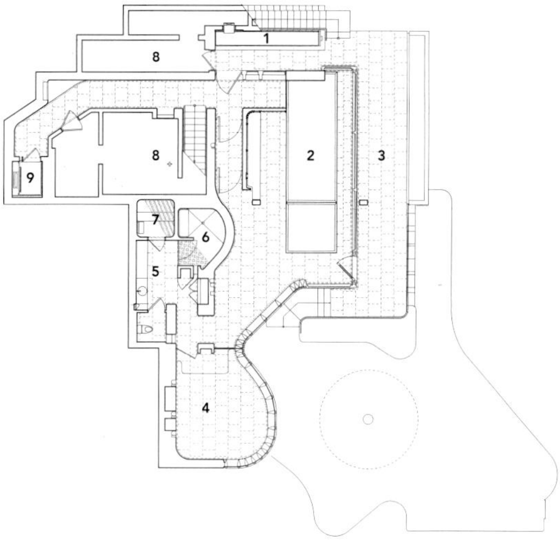

LEVEL 1

1 fountain
2 pool
3 terrace
4 exercise room
5 change room
6 shower/steam room
7 sauna
8 mechanical room
9 elevator

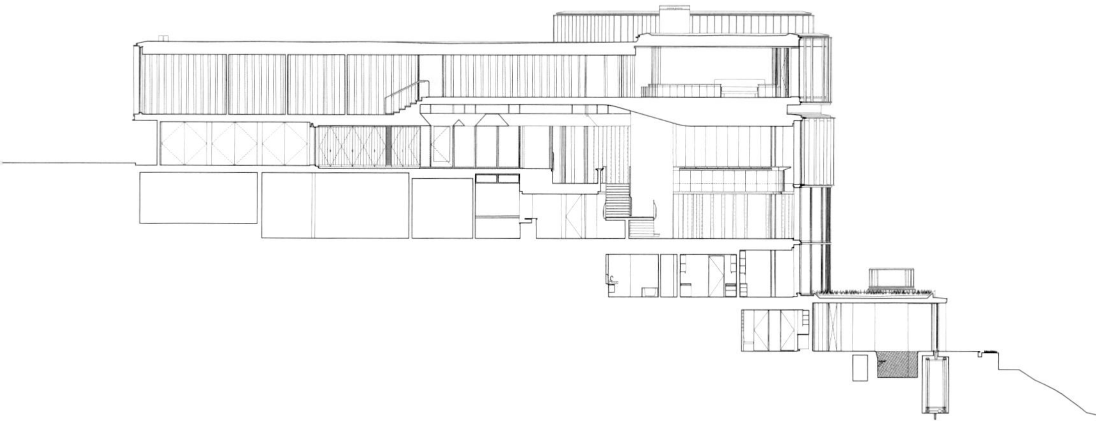

The design of the detail has been pursued in the Integral House by developing a vocabulary of hardware elements and railings. Conceived as lines that articulate space and movement, balustrades with cast bronze vertical supports that carry leather wrapped handrails and stainless steel mesh form a smaller architecture within the whole. The handrail designs vary depending on their location and importance in the project. A custom handle has also been developed for the house using both traditional modeling techniques and computer generated rapid prototyping. The design of the handle was initiated in our studio using clay. In collaboration with Betsy and Shane Williamson, these handmade models were drawn digitally in three dimensions and then precisely modeled by a 3D printer. Cast in bronze, the handle is contoured to the hand and the placement of the thumb; the form captures the rotation of the wrist.

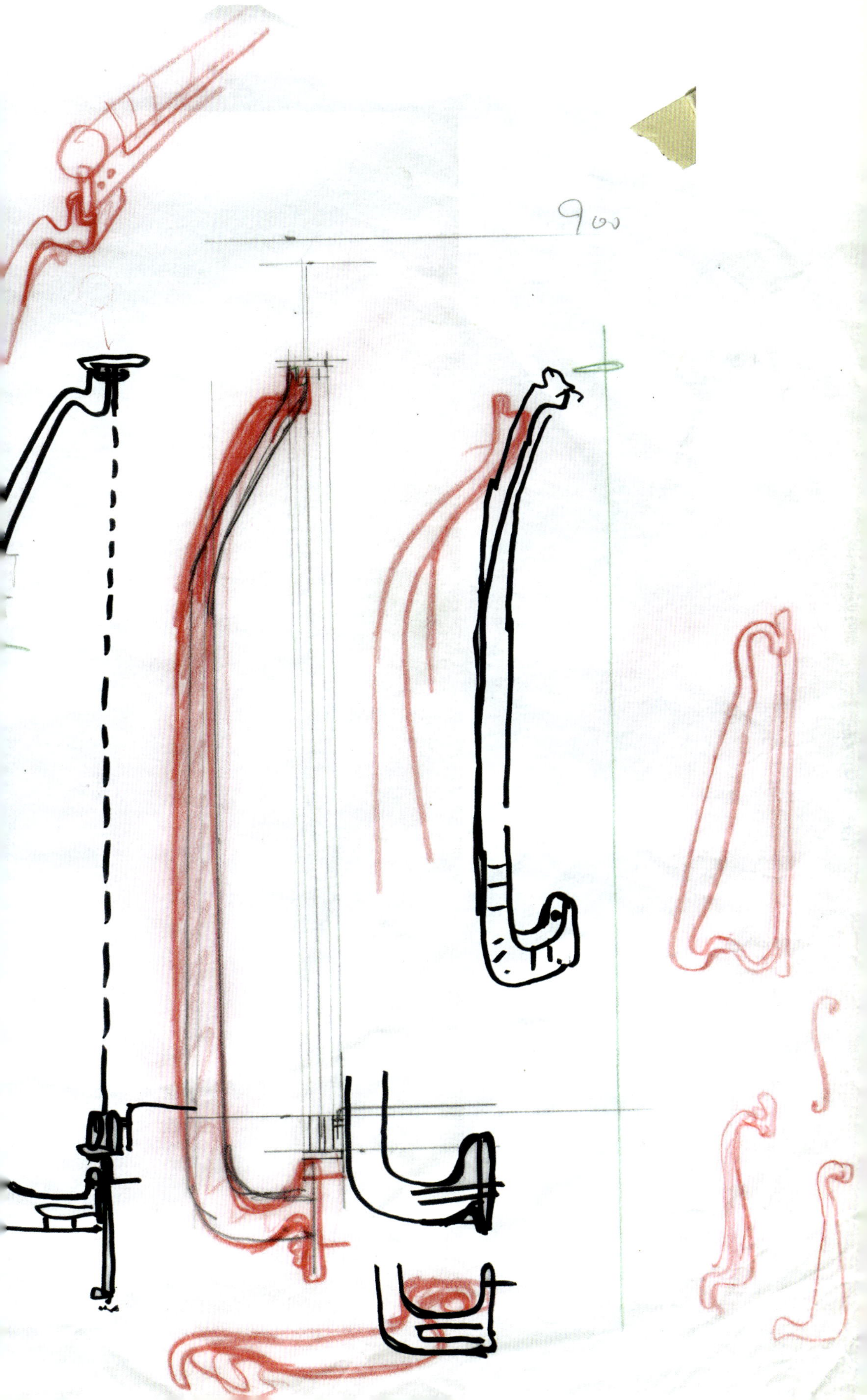
900

Carved edges of the floor and ceiling planes, held away from the fin wall, are detailed to reinforce the curving perimeter. The house will have a stone baseboard, which bounds the edge of the floor and distinguishes it from the screen of wooden fins. The curved stone pieces are computer generated shapes fabricated by CNC milling machines. Similarly, the two free-standing columns in the main living and performance space have evolved through a series of drawings and models that explore both the technical and visual aspects of the structure and examine how they are wrapped with an oak skin. In contrast to the planar sense of the walls and the mass of the concrete shafts, these finer-scale elements are tuned to the human touch yet, at a small scale, reiterate the ideas and themes of the larger project.

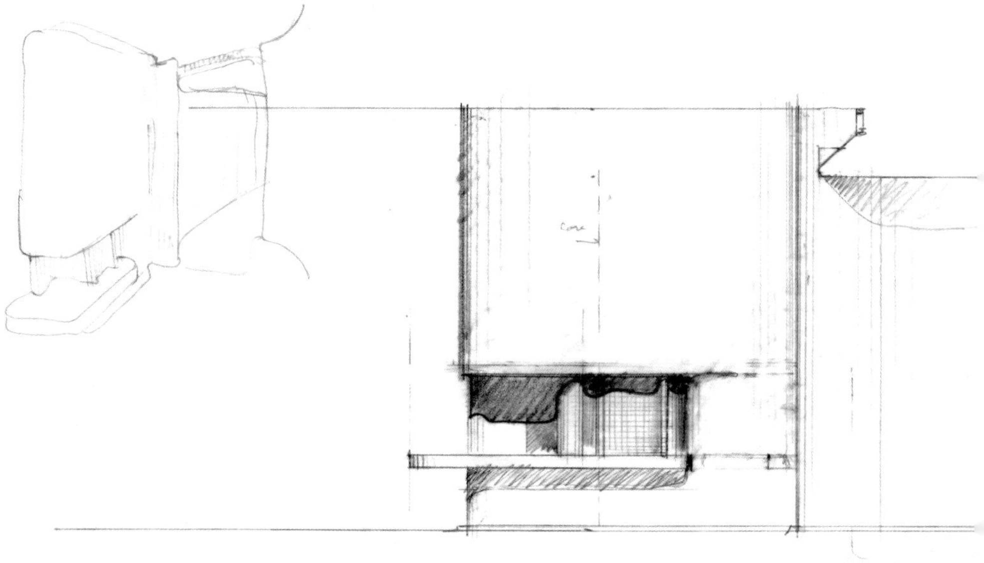

Studies of the fireplaces develop the idea of figural masses within the space. Formally resonating with the organic nature of the space itself, these concentrated undulating elements focus toward the interior. The fireplaces, which are stacked above each other, occur in the family room, dining room and master bedroom. In each case, they are composed within the U-shaped frame of the concrete mass that punctures the floor slabs on the south side of the living spaces. They are designed with striated layers of materials and curvatures that help define the 'program' of the fireplace. The line of the stone hearth projects into the space, while an upper plaster volume curves back against the flues. The mantle, detailed in architectural bronze, forms a mediating line between these two elements.

The fireboxes are lined with the same stainless steel mesh that forms the balustrades – a mesh that creates a consistent horizontal datum that passes through the house with various degrees of opacity. At the fireplaces, the mesh is dense. It folds into the fireboxes and wood storage areas, where it becomes a supple stainless steel ribbon that echoes the undulating form of the exterior wall.

The pool of the Integral House is developed conceptually as a space carved out within the forest floor. It is composed of simple elements – a horizontal plane of water, a vertical plane of marble, and a bench of wood alongside. The pool surface is a pure plane of water set at the level of the floor. A 15 mm gap at the top of a carved coping edge allows the overflow to fall smoothly into a hidden channel. The tautness of this plane and the dark gray limestone of the pool liner – the same stone as the floor – create a highly reflective surface for the Connemara marble wall and the ravine forest that is immediately adjacent to this space. The pool becomes an intensely horizontal space within a very vertical house and provides a panoramic view of a slice of the ravine. The figured green marble works as an abstract landscape with light passing over it, illuminating both the marble and its reflection in the pool. The openness of the landscape next to the pool is reinforced by a large floor-to-ceiling glass window that sits on a beam that is raised and lowered by four stainless steel screw jacks. In one motion, the 35 foot-long window drops into the floor, to completely disappear and open the room into the ravine.

The figural character of the Integral House is more pronounced than in our previous work, but this is not new territory. Many of our projects have modest figural components. The leaf roof of the garden pavilion is an enigmatic element that contrasts with the orthogonal language of the retaining walls in the landscape, and the wood ceiling of the Muskoka Boathouse, like a soft fabric, is embedded in the robust heavy timber construction. There are obvious references to Alvar Aalto in the Integral House, both in the relationship of orthogonal and organic formal languages and in the details. We did not think about it consciously when we were designing the project, but there are also many ways in which the scheme refers to the work of Le Corbusier. Like the Carpenter Center and the Millowners Association Building in Ahmedabad, the free plan is anchored by strong figural elements and enclosed by thick, light modulating walls. Together with a studio we have just completed in Toronto and a synagogue we are designing in Maine, the Integral House is one of a group of projects in which we are exploring thick walls as light modulators. In the Craven Road Studio, a free-standing studio which serves as a research, exhibition and display area for an archivist, a system of narrow light coffers surrounds the entire perimeter of the space, varying in both rhythm and depth depending on orientation. The incoming light washes across the face of the wood fins providing warmth and a glow that is only possible with this articulated section.

Most of our projects are polychromatic to balance the colors of the natural materials that we use. We rarely use white. The vertical concrete shaft that is embedded in the orthogonal zone of the house contains a blue glass-lined stair, which was developed at the outset of the project in collaboration with the artist Mimi Gellman. The stair seeks to blur the distinction between architecture and art. To understand the transition from dark blue at the bottom of the stair to light blue at the top as well as the potential of light coming from above onto this blue glass wall, we made many drawings, models and large-scale mock-ups. Rectangular shingles of laminated double-flashed hand blown glass in shades of blue are carried by sand-cast bronze clips on a stainless steel rod and cable system designed to float free of the concrete walls.

The cables span from the laser-cut steel tread supports to the perimeter of the laylight structure. Laminated translucent glass treads allow light to filter down from the skylight to the lower levels of the house. In contrast with the grand entry stair, which focuses on the descent into the ravine and the opening up of the external wall to the woods, the experience of the second stair within the concrete shaft is introverted. Within this stair, the abstract quality of 'blueness' is important. All other details will be suppressed to focus on the colored glass illuminated by both natural and artificial light. Blue light will spill out through slits in the concrete shaft to illuminate rooms around the stair on various levels, which are the more private spaces of the house.

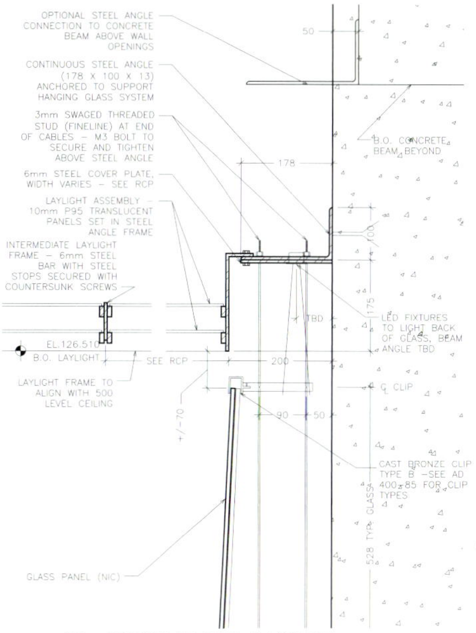

1 SECTION AT STAIR 6 LAYLIGHT
Scale: 1:5

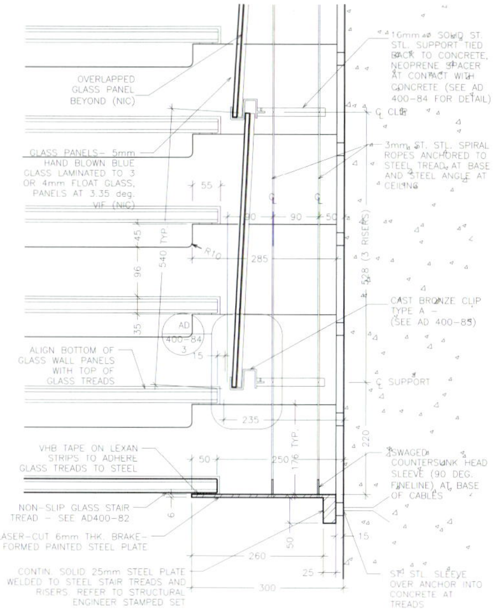

2 SECTION AT STAIR TREAD
Scale: 1:5

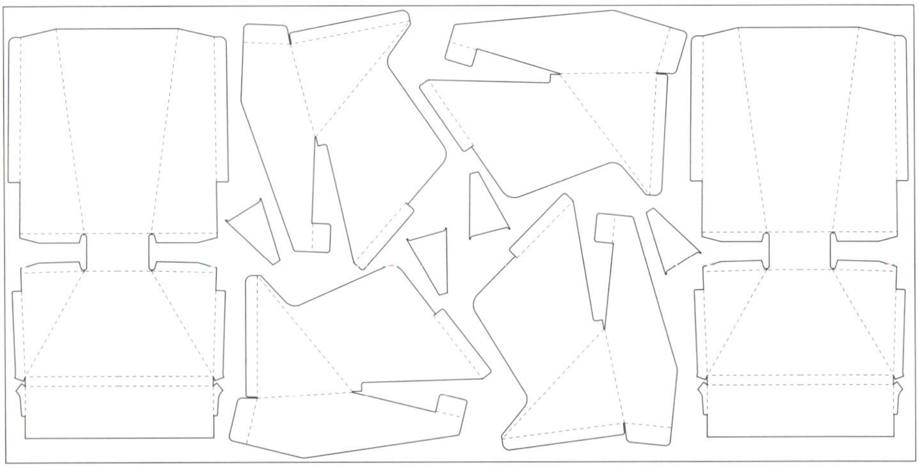

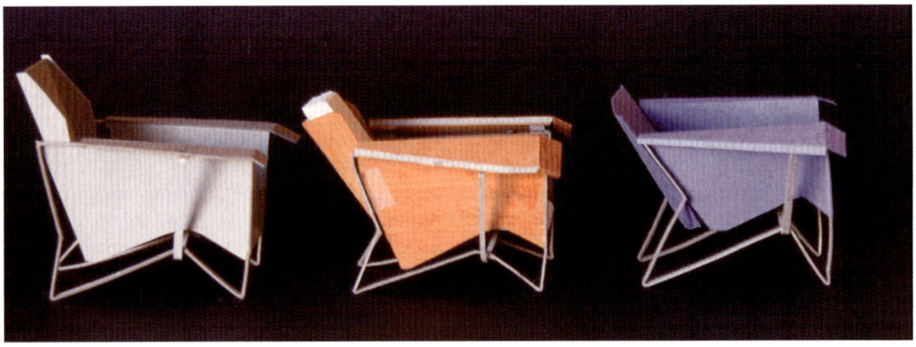

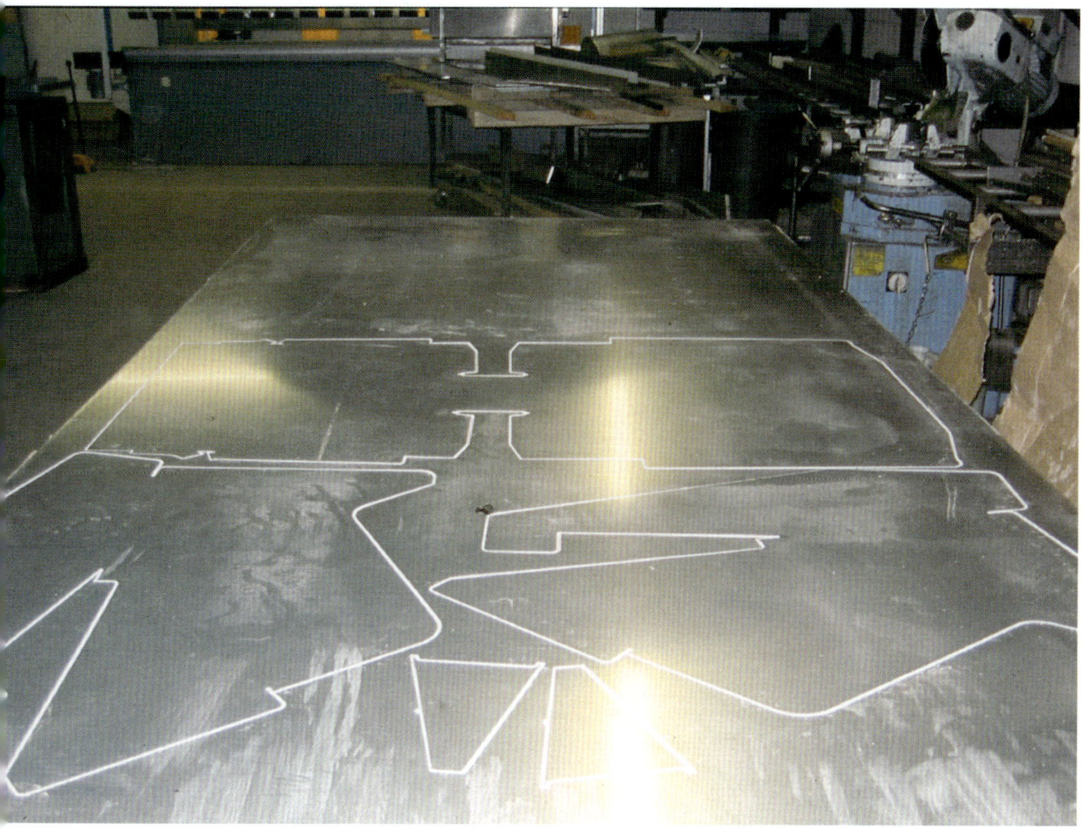

Because we like to make things, we feel everything we draw should ideally be something we could make ourselves. We think about how every detail is going to be made. With computers, this exercise can be much more precise and we can achieve a level of accuracy that would not be possible if the detail was being made using only traditional tools. When we designed and built our first project, Howard drew lines on a sheet of steel that was to become the roof of the garden pavilion and then flame cut it himself at the steel fabricator's shop. The relationship between design and making was direct.

For the Muskoka Boathouse we designed a chair that was built by a custom millwork fabricator. We were subsequently asked to develop the design as a manufactured version, which is now being made by Klaus Nienkamper and distributed across North America. I am short and Howard is tall. We decided the chair had to be comfortable for both of us, which is a difficult task. The construction of full size cardboard models of the chair made it possible to produce prototypes in different materials including bamboo and fiberglass.

For a year, all of the visitors to our studio had to sit in the chair and tell us what did and did not work for them. We refined the dimensions accordingly and then made a series of molds using vacuum-forming equipment. The final chair has a stainless steel frame and a body of either maple or aluminum, both of which are laser cut from sheet material.

The Integral House is much larger and more complex, so we have clearly had to work in a different way. While we worked with chipboard and tracing paper study models in the early stages of the design process, the computer is fundamental to its fabrication and construction. We have used digital processes more on this project than on any other. From the outset, the curved wall was designed to be produced digitally. With conventional drafting techniques, it would have been extremely difficult to describe some of the conditions that have been developed in the undulating wall. Without the computer, the geometric complexity of locating all the points of this wall in space would be very demanding.

Employing every technique at our disposal, from traditional hand to digital design and fabrication, we always try to use the lowest form of technology that is

appropriate at each stage of the project. We use many different kinds of experience and forms of representation and production as we collaborate to develop ideas. We suggested to Jim that he live in the existing house on the site before it was demolished. He spent a year there to gain an understanding of the changing light and seasons. After he left, Howard worked in the empty house for a month and together we laid out the new house with tape on the floors.

In developing the construction documents, we had to do a setting out drawing for ourselves that would precisely define the curved wall as well as locate and shape every fin. Having done this, we realized that this drawing could be fabricated at full scale, creating a laser cut steel template for the whole building with the survey grid engraved on it that would be extremely accurate. The basement foundations were built up from this *summa* line template. However, it is not part of the final project and was only made and used to locate components of the building. When the concrete shafts and slabs were finally in place, the steel template was replaced by laser cut plywood templates around the perimeter of each floor, which are engraved with details guiding the installation of the glass and the wooden fins. These wood templates will remain embedded, but unseen, in the final assembly. In the history of architecture there are all kinds of devices that were necessary to make a building, but which are tools that disappear after it is built. As architects, we often do not think about these elements when we are designing, but they are essential to construction.

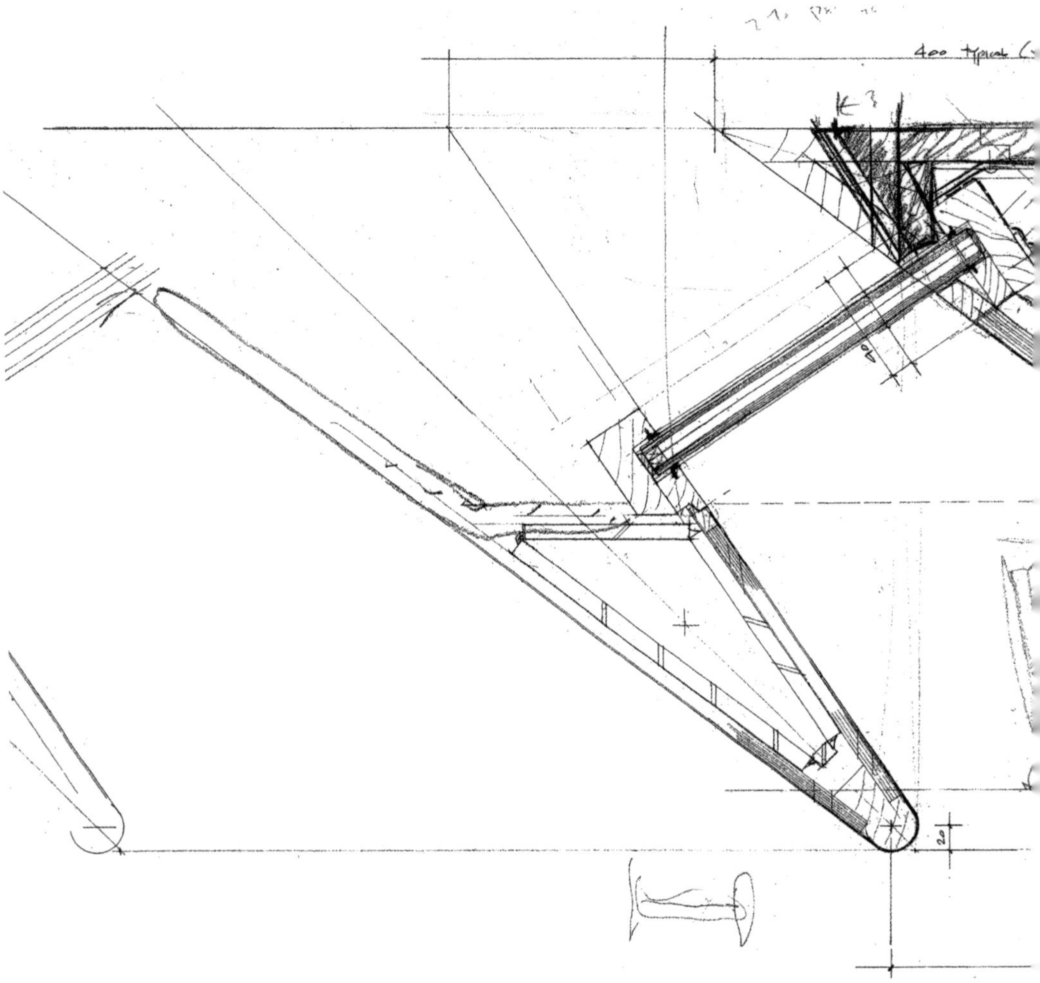

To develop the window fins we worked with fabricators in Toronto and studied the detail through a series of full scale mock-ups. The wall is labor intensive, with each individual fin and window being a substantial and detailed body of work. Each fin is shaped to sculpt light as it enters the space, and the series of fins follows the curved line of the house. Consequently, each fin is a different size and shape. The fin locations and profiles were precisely defined, then translated to CNC fabricated templates and structural forms directly from our computer drawings. The wood window manufacturer and site carpenters then fitted and shaped the custom millwork covers to the fabricated pieces. While the wall was initially designed using conventional techniques, its fabrication was based in computer driven processes.

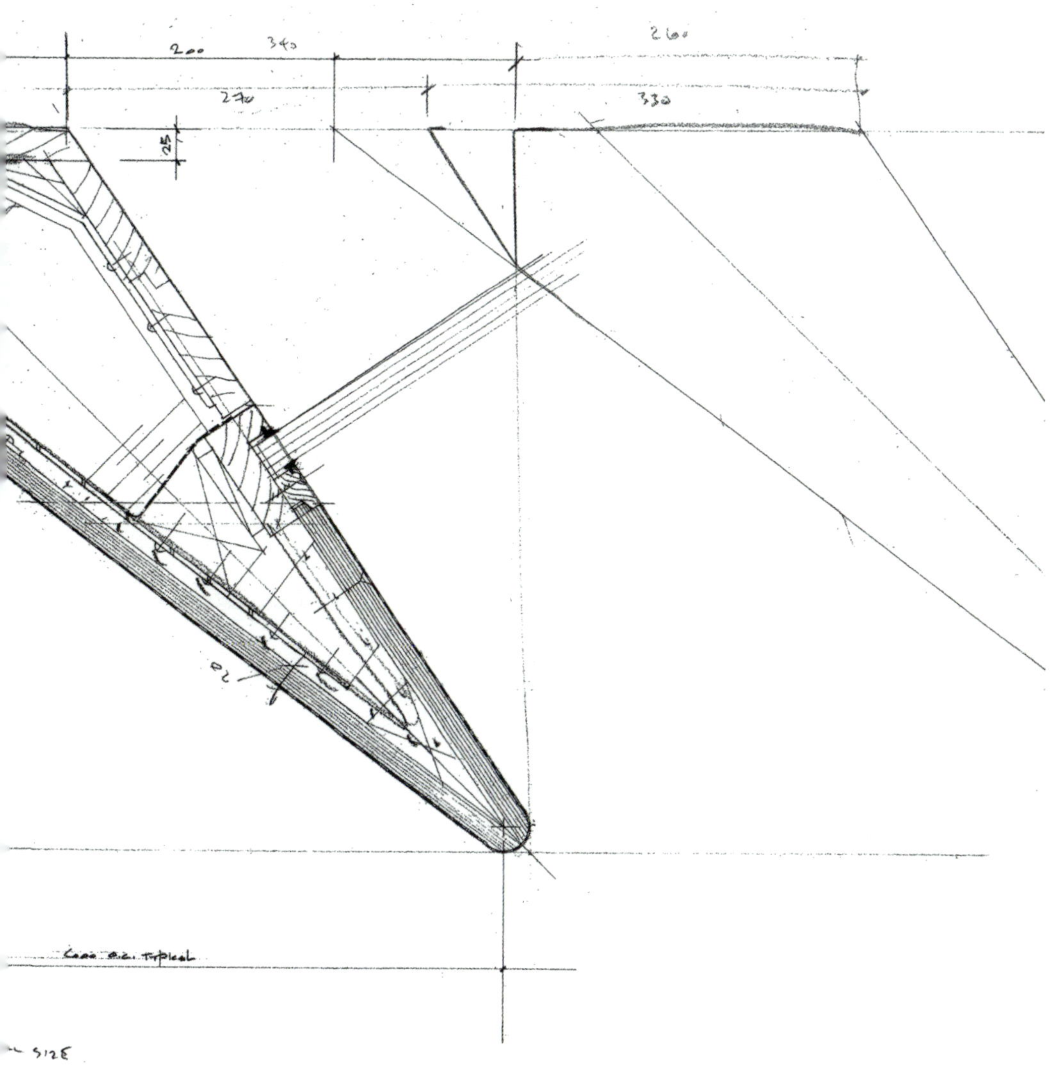
200
340
260
270
330
25
typical
SIZE

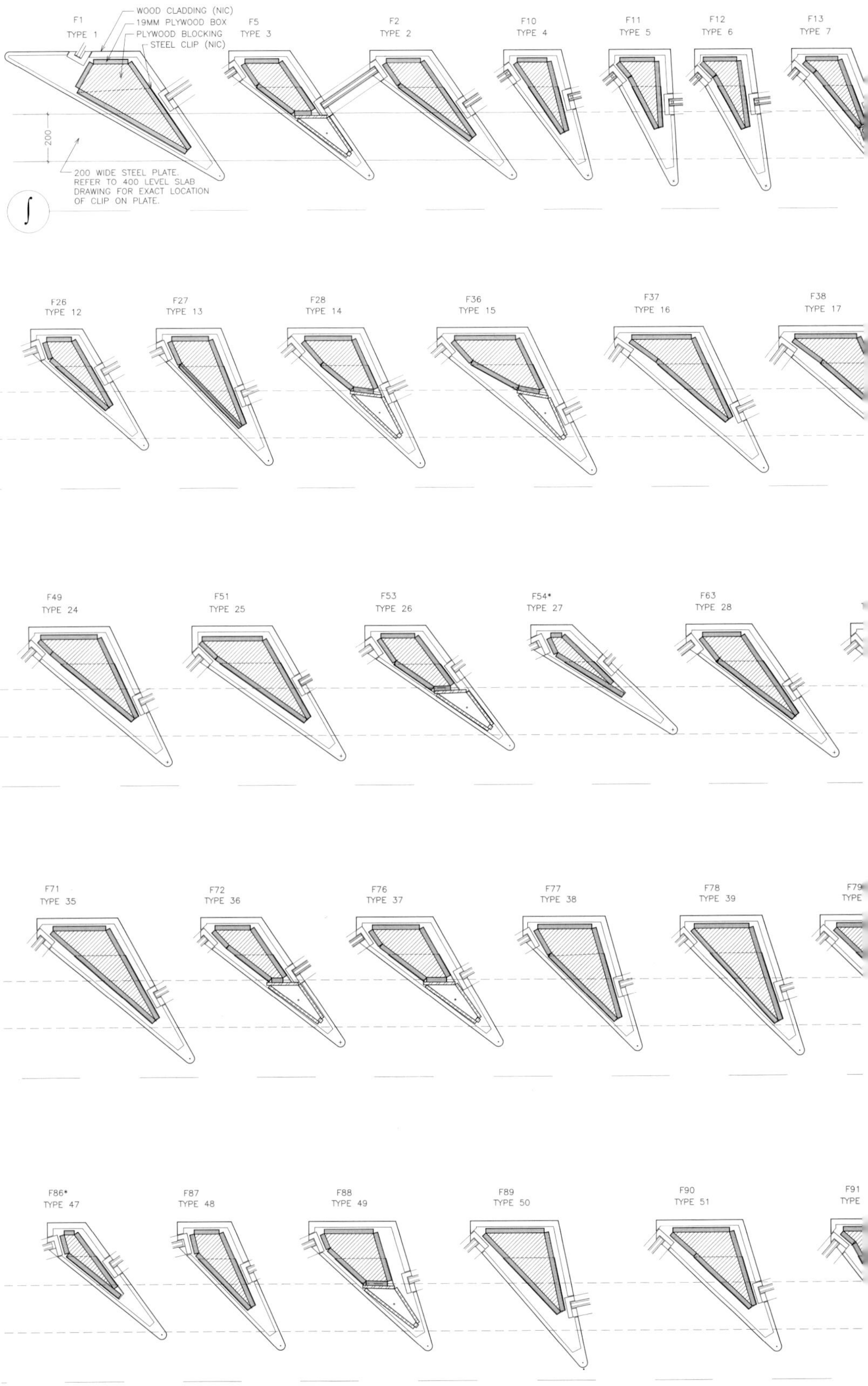

F1
TYPE 1
WOOD CLADDING (NIC)
19MM PLYWOOD BOX
PLYWOOD BLOCKING
STEEL CLIP (NIC)
200
200 WIDE STEEL PLATE.
REFER TO 400 LEVEL SLAB
DRAWING FOR EXACT LOCATION
OF CLIP ON PLATE.
F5
TYPE 3
F2
TYPE 2
F10
TYPE 4
F11
TYPE 5
F12
TYPE 6
F13
TYPE 7
F26
TYPE 12
F27
TYPE 13
F28
TYPE 14
F36
TYPE 15
F37
TYPE 16
F38
TYPE 17
F49
TYPE 24
F51
TYPE 25
F53
TYPE 26
F54*
TYPE 27
F63
TYPE 28
F71
TYPE 35
F72
TYPE 36
F76
TYPE 37
F77
TYPE 38
F78
TYPE 39
F86*
TYPE 47
F87
TYPE 48
F88
TYPE 49
F89
TYPE 50
F90
TYPE 51
F91

F19 TYPE 9 | F20 TYPE 10 | F21 TYPE 11 | F24 TYPE 60 | F25 TYPE 59

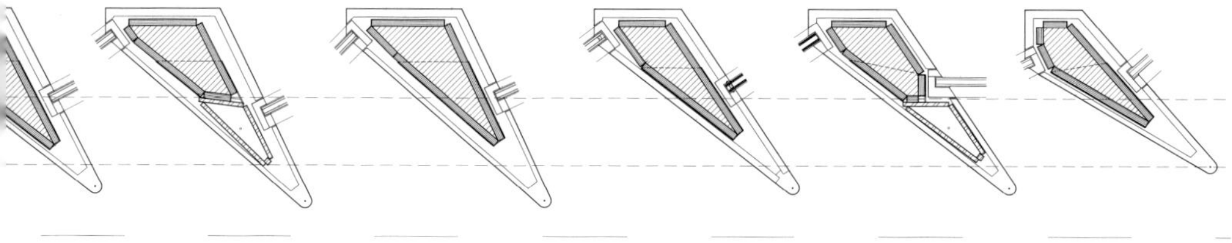

F44 TYPE 19 | F45 TYPE 20 | F46 TYPE 21 | F47 TYPE 22 | F48 TYPE 23

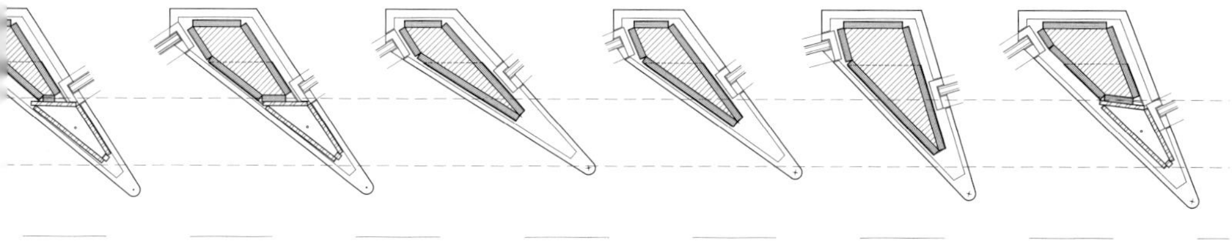

F65 TYPE 30 | F66 TYPE 31 | F67 TYPE 32 | F68 TYPE 33 | F69 TYPE 34

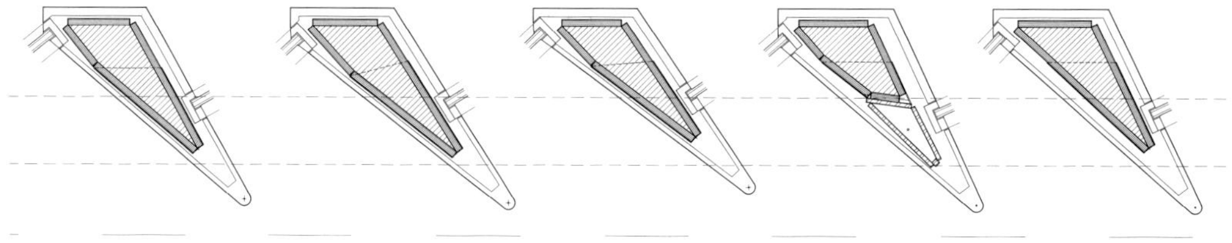

0 E 41 | F81* TYPE 42 | F82* TYPE 43 | F83* TYPE 44 | F84* TYPE 45 | F85* TYPE 46

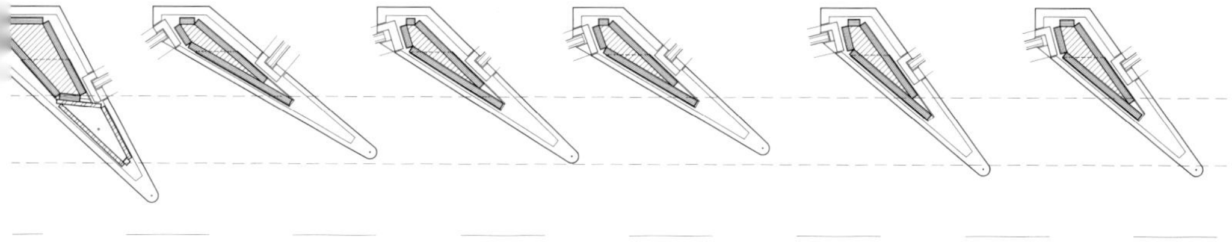

F93* TYPE 54 | F94* TYPE 55 | F95 TYPE 56 | F96 TYPE 57 | F97 TYPE 58

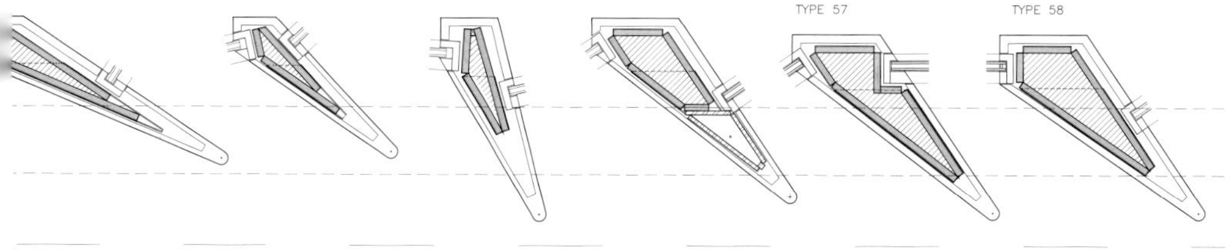

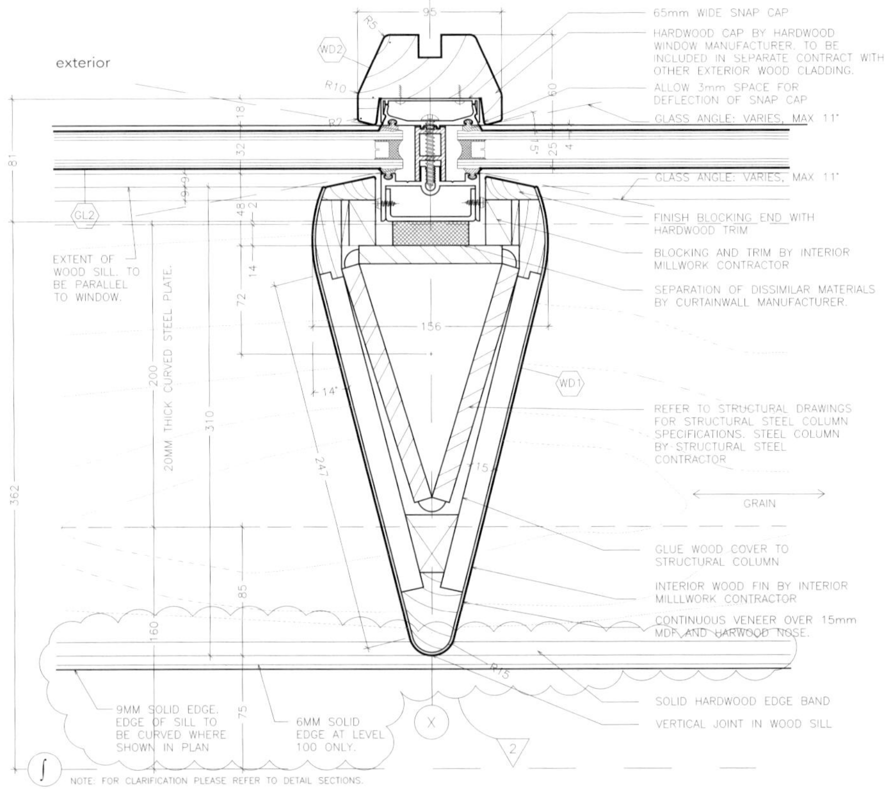

Structural expression has never been a primary interest for us. In the Integral House, the concrete fireplace, elevator and stair shafts provide lateral restraint. In order to reduce the need for free-standing structural support for the concrete slabs, small triangular steel columns were designed that could be incorporated within the curtain wall system. Because these columns are very slender, they can accept no moment forces and are connected to the slab with a fully rotational pin connection. Around the perimeter of the plan, the steel plate columns are closely spaced at approximately 2400 mm centers. The columns are continuous through all levels, but the placement of the fins differs from floor to floor. These perimeter columns will be concealed within the wood fins. In the finished project, it will not be obvious which fins are structural and which are not. This distinction will evaporate. The suppression of the literal structure of the perimeter wall shifts the emphasis to more significant terrain for us, underlining the way in which this wall structures the entire project phenomenologically.

In the Integral House, the thick wall as a light modulator transcends the figural attributes of the form. Much of the design effort of this project has consequently been focused on the three window systems that make up the perimeter glazing screen. Each of these systems has a different degree of transparency and enclosure and provides a distinct relationship between the occupant and the landscape. The lower three levels are clad in a customized curtain wall, millwork and structural fin system that occupies a zone that is approximately 300 mm deep.

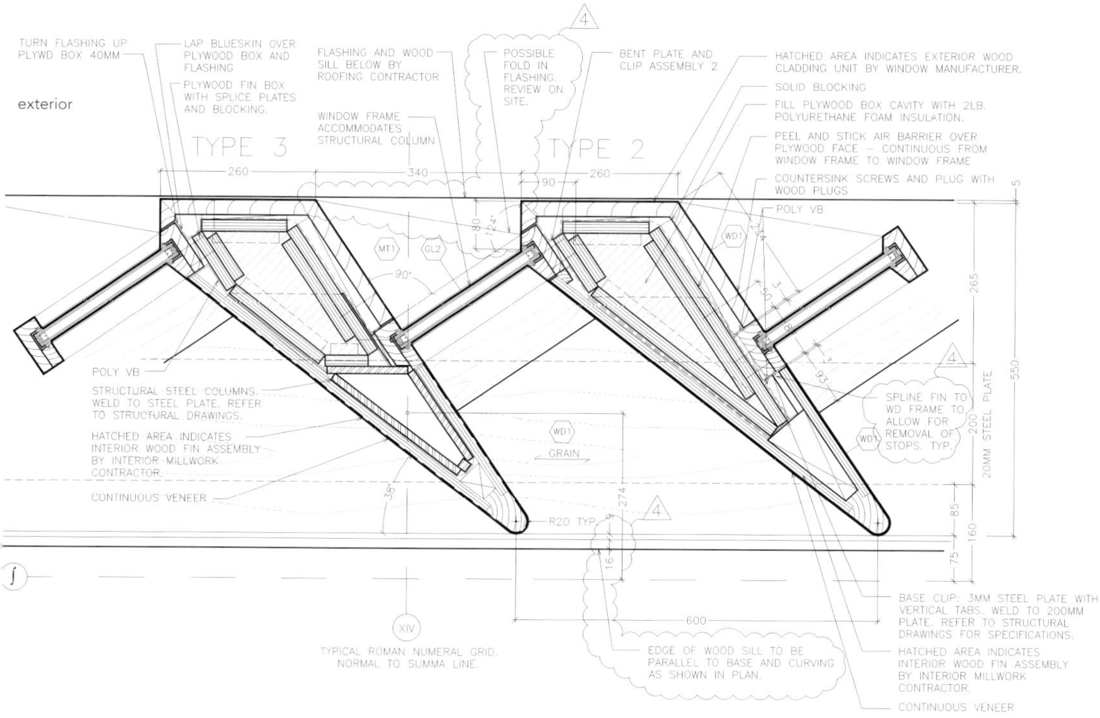

The second system is the glass and wood fin enclosure at the entry level floor, which is 550 mm deep. Visually, these deeper fins provide much more enclosure and control of views than the first system. Depending on one's perspective and path of movement through the house, the system can vary from appearing completely opaque to transparent. In places, it is possible to stand between fins within the thickness of the light-modulating wall. In another current project for a gatehouse, the external wall becomes even thicker so that, in addition to baffling light, it houses spaces that become fully occupiable.

These two external wall systems are designed as a typical module of triangular fin and canted glass window. As at the lower levels, the millwork enclosure hides both the structure and the window frame, allowing a pure reading of wood and glass that softens the light washing across the surface. From the inside, you will see only wood and view, and the fin wall will almost feel as if it is open to the ravine. The exterior frame is clad with an Ipe cap that will be left to weather to a soft gray to blend with the tree trunks in the ravine. Responding to the complex issue of property lines and limiting distances, the fins cant as they move around the perimeter. Because they are always oriented perpendicular to the curved edge of the floor plate and have nosings that are spaced equally apart, they developed unique profiles to moderate these two conditions. The fins thicken at the outside curves and become thinner at the inside curves so as to reinforce the undulation of the wall.

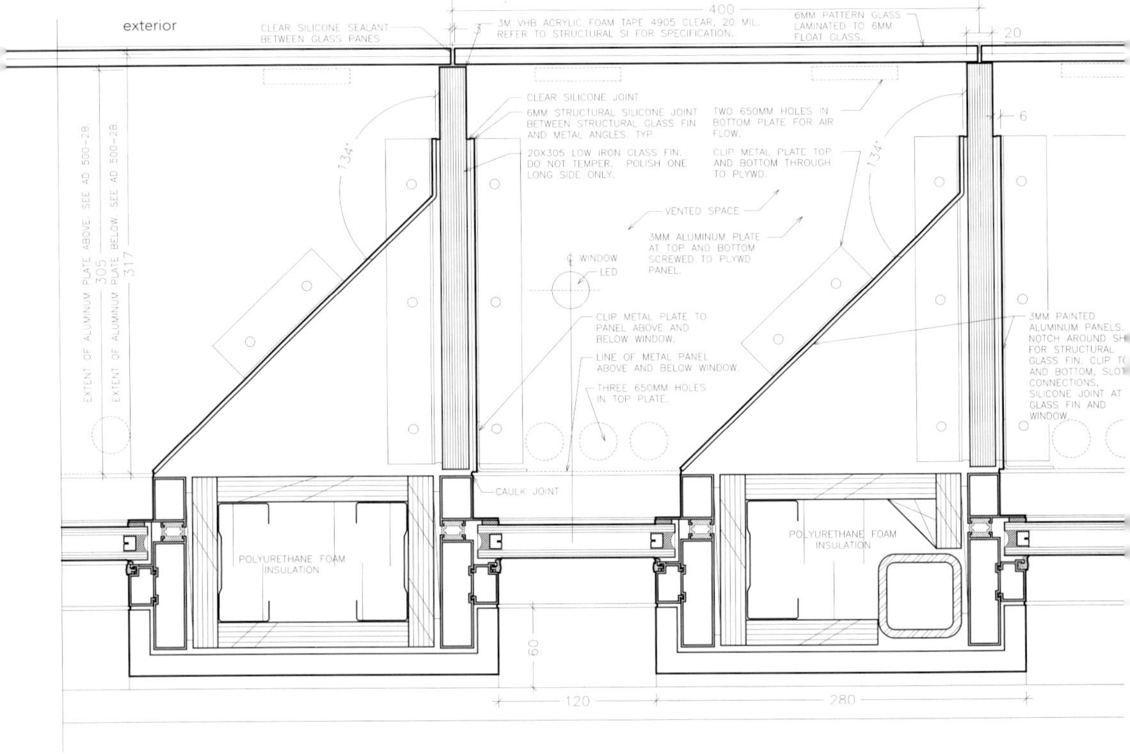

The top floor of the house is largely clad in a third external wall system, almost a reversal of those below, which will read as a continuous, monolithic and spatially deep surface. Here, aluminum clad fins with clear weathertight glazing near the inner face will be wrapped in a rainscreen of frameless translucent glass, which works as a scrim that ties all of the vertical elements of the house together. At night, this floating surface will be lighted from within by LEDs to give the house the soft glow of an Akari lamp and an ethereal presence within the ravine.

Reading the brief at the outset, it was clear that, for our mathematician client, the curve was fundamental to his thinking. Consequently, it has been important to us to find a way to make it an essential part of the design. The curve creates challenges at every level but, with computers, the relationship between the design idea and its implementation through fabrication offers new potential. This project has provided a laboratory that is enabling us to explore new territory as architects. We have conceived the Integral House as a place that will become a home for our client. We hope that the final built work will allow him to continue to look, learn and think about the spaces that surround him and engage both the natural and fabricated world.

Ed Burtynsky, a significant international artist and environmentalist, has been inventing and refining techniques for making photographs for more than twenty years. His remarkable body of work has explored subjects such as the Three River Gorges Dam in mainland China and the shipwreckers of Bangladesh. He visits the new beauty spots in the world – quarries, oil fields and recycling plants.

Prior to construction of the Integral House commencing on site, Ed placed a camera in a tree in the ravine to record the process of demolition and construction of a new building on the site by taking a photograph every ten minutes throughout the year. This reading of the construction process of the Integral House through the discerning lens of Ed's camera has captured key stages of the project's development. The observation of demolition and construction over the course of time evokes simultaneously a vanishing and emerging presence. By offering a perspective on the transformation of this site in the ravine, the images also record the messy grittiness of the construction process, which is easy to forget. Unlike published images of finished buildings, these images are an intermediary that describes the human effort involved in bringing a building into existence. This is a demanding process and one that consumes much of our attention and energy as architects. Yet at the same time, when this building is finished, we hope it will appear inevitable, as if it has always been there.

	ARCHITECTS
Shim·Sutcliffe Architects inc.	BRIGITTE SHIM & HOWARD SUTCLIFFE, Principals BETSY WILLIAMSON, Project Architect MIKE GOOREVICH ANDREW HART DENISE HARADEM KYRA CLARKSON SARAH IWATA ELENA CHERNYSHOV THEO KELADITIS, Model Maker APRIL WONG, Model Maker
	CONSULTANTS
Structural Engineer	DAVID BOWICK, Blackwell Bowick Partnership IAN MOUNTFORT SHAUKAT ALI GRAZYNA CZARNECKA GREG SAWKA SHANNON HILCHIE PAULINA HERRERA CHRIS CUCCO REZA MIKHCHIAN
Mechanical Engineer	FRANK TOEWS, Toews Engineering PETER GRANT MILIND LIKHITE BRIAN MCEWEN TERRY MAK SHELLEY SEQUIN
Electrical Engineer	TONY MONOPOLI, Dynamic Designs and Engineering Inc.
Landscape Architecture	ROBERT NG, NAK Design Group LI CHENZI SIMON YUE KATHY ZIELINSKI
Building Envelope Consultant	DR. TED KESIK, University of Toronto
Lighting Consultant	SUZANNE POWADIUK, Suzanne Powadiuk Design Inc.
Interior Design	JULIE LATRAVERSE, Drummond LaTraverse Interior Design CHRIS OLIVER, Decisive Moment Incorporated
Digital fabrication consultant	SHANE WILLIAMSON, WilliamsonWilliamson
Code Consultant	DAVE HINE, Hine Reichard Tomlin Inc. RYAN NORTH
Planning Consultant	ADAM BROWN, Sherman Brown Dryer Karol
Plan Examiner	MARCUS AREGAWI, City of Toronto
Plan Review Manager	PRABHAKAR MAHANT, City of Toronto
Fountain Consultant	DAN EUSER, Waterarchitecture Inc.
Acoustical Engineer, Mechanical System	JOHN SWALLOW, Swallow Acoustic Consultants Limited FRANK BABIC MIHKEL TOOME
Glass engineer	DAVE PROHASKA, DT Prohaska Engineering

COLLABORATORS

Artist	ED BURTYNSKY, Toronto Image Works MARCUS SCHUBERT CHARLES ROULEAU NOAH WEINZWEIG
Artist	MIMI GELLMAN

CONTRACTORS

General Contractor	STEVE EISNER & STEVE MURRAY, Eisner Murray, Principals VIC FURGIUELE, Construction Manager FRASER WILLOUGHBY, Carpenter IAN SCHWIEN, Carpenter MARK LEWIS, Carpenter AL TONEGUZZI, Carpenter IOURI SEVOSTIANOV, Carpenter STEVE CORRIGAN, Carpenter ROBERT HILLER, Carpenter JIM MARSHALL, Carpenter LISA RENDELY, Site Intern
Advanced Coatings Inc.	VLADIMIR VICIC, Owner MIKE DUPUIS, Installer DEREK ARTHURUS, Installer
Alar-Vac	SAM SABRI, Project Manager MAJID JALILIAN, Installer
Amherst Crane Rentals Ltd.	PAT HAGGART, Project Manager
Anchor Shoring Caissons Ltd.	PAUL KREYCIR, Owner MIKE LESAGE, Supervisor CHRIS AITKEN ANSON AUSTIN PHILIP CARPENTER LUIS CARVALHO PAUL EDWARDS JAMES GRIFFIN TREVOR HIGGINS FREEMAN HUTCHINGS CHAD HYNES WILLIAM JEWELL DALE LE CLAIR DENNIS MACWHIRTER JAMES MCGRATH DAN PAUL ERNESTO REGO TONY STACK STEVE STANISIC JOHN THOMPSON
Applewood Glass and Mirror Inc.	ANTHONY MENECOLA, Owner NICK GOSCHY, Project Estimator RAVI SENANAYAKE, Project Co-ordinator KELLY RYAN, Project Site Foreman
Applied Industrial Floor Systems	SALEH MOUSSA DARI, Installer KHALID SOULEYMAN, Installer
Automation Engineering Associates Ltd.	JOHN PAUL FAICZAK, Project Manager TONY MA, Site Foreman MAHMOUD ELGEBALI, Software
Avante Security Inc.	MANNY MOUNOUCHOS, President KARNIG NAZARETIAN, Project Manager ALEX FOLLIS, Installer LEONCIO GUILLEN, Installer DEREK MAVUWA, Installer
Avenue Building Corporation	CORRADO PATULLO, Owner TONY PATULLO, Owner CARMINE PATULLO, Owner JIM PATULLO, Project Manager MARK BOSSA, Project Manager MANUEL RIBEIRO, Foreman ALEXANDER ARANIBAR FERDINANDO BATTOCCHIO

JOSE CUSTODIO
RENATO DA SILVA
ANTONIO FERNANDES
TIAGO GOMES
VIRGILIO GOMES
ANDELINO GONCALVES
IAN GOURLAY
FERNANDO MARQUES
ANTONIO MIGNELLA
EMANUEL MONCADA
RICARDO MORIM
MANUEL RIBEIRO

BerCool Mechanial Ltd.	ERIC PESCE, Owner NABIL HADDAD, Project Manager CLAUDIO PESCE, Site Supervisor HAMED AHANI KEN SIMPSON
CB Marble Craft Limited	ARMIE LEONETTI, Site Superintendent DAVID BERTOLLI, Aministration PATRICK BERTOLLI, Production CLAUDIA COLUSSI, Office Manager JAMES PURI, Project Co-ordinator AL PELLIZZONI, Installer DAVID PELLIZZONI, Installer ALEX DOBROWOLSKI, Installer
C.E. Dotterill Ltd. Surveyors	BRAD WARREN RAY KALNINS DAVID MARTIN NICK SZOPIAK BARRY WALKER
Ciot Toronto Inc.	FERNANDO MAMMOLITI, Owner
Construction Concrete Tiles	JOSE CARLOS, Installer DANIEL DASILVA, Installer
Craftwood Custom Millwork	GARY SONNENBERG, Owner KEVIN LOTT, Engineer, Project manager JEFF LIEBOLD, Engineer, Project manager PETER SAWALA, Estimator
D'Ales Construction Co.	BRUNO D'ALESSANDRO, Owner and Installer
Dazit Production Technology	MICHAEL NOGA, Superior Intech Inc., Engineering RICHARD HINTERHOELLER, Superior Intech Inc., Engineering BILL BOYKO, Techserv TSI, Sales TERRY BOYKO, Techserv TSI, Project Management NOEL MCDOUGALL, Techserv TSI, Project Management BILL SNOW, Techserv TSI, On-site Supervisor TO HA MACH, Machining, On-site Installation BRETT PATTERSON, Bretco Electric Inc., Electric Controls RON BESSEY, Ralm Electrical Millwrights Inc., On-site Mechanical Installation ED SOUZA, C.M. Morris Design, Machining JIM BRAUN, C.M. Morris Design, Machining DAN MARIN, Pro Finish Equipment Services, Sand Blast and Painting
DeRock Electric	GEORGE DEFRANCESCA, Owner, ME, Site Supervisor ROCCO PILLA, Owner ELSIE HIRSCHIND, Office Administrator ROBERT PILLA, Service Manager SANDRO CACCAMO, Electrician, Site Foreman SHAWN BAKER, Electrician KEN LAU, Electrician CARLOS CALADO, Electrician ANDREW DEFRANCESCA, Apprentice QUINN O'CONNELL, Apprentice
Downsview Drywall Contractors	EUGENE CONTE, Project Manager JOHN CHRISSIKOS, Supervisor
Duffy and Associates	ANDREW DUFFY
Enviroturf	TREVER PRENEVOST, Operations Manager JEFF ROBERTS, Service Supervisor JIM MACMILLAN, Service Technician TIM OSBORNE, Service Technician

Federal Elevator	JOHN RAE, Project Coordinator
Fulton Windows	EHAB NAIM IBRAHIM, Technical Consultant
Gabor Kirschner Painting	GABOR KIRSCHNER, Owner ATTILA HORVATH
Gamma Foundries Company	GARY BUNYAN
Gingers Bath Center	ROSALIE LEVINE, Sales Representative
GWS Foam Insulation	WAYNE COONS, Owner and Installer ADAM COONS, Installer
Harris Rebar	IVAN MIKESIC, Detailer
Haddad Geotechnical Inc.	GRAHAM FISHER ALLEN BERTRAN MUHAMMAD MAQSOOD ABDUL SHUKOORI
Hermanns Landscape Contracting Ltd.	JORG HERMANN, Owner GERD HERMANN, Owner GORD KERR, Project Manager MIKE TAYLOR RICK JOSLIN JOHN TOBIN TORY HODGSON RAY MARSHALL PETER KAMSTRA BARB ELLISON SHANNON WICKLER KULWANT DEV HAKIM DHALIWAL
Khanadian Metal Fabrication	ABDOOL HAFEEZ KHAN, Owner and Project Manager MAHDI SABERI DUONG TRUNG NGHIA ARMIN FOCIC BOGDAN JANJUSEVIC
Leak Free Caulking	DAVID MACIUK, Owner and Installer FRANK CASTRO, Installer
Mariani Metal Fabricators Limited	VINCE MARIANI, Owner ANDRE LEON, MARIANI METAL, Project Manager TONY D'ADDARIO, Estimator DOUG ALEXANDER, Detailer ANGELO D'ASCANIA LARRY DUBEK TONY ANZELOTTI
Oldcastle Glass	DONOVAN HARTY OLIVER LUMBER IAN SMART
Omico Mechanical Ltd.	LOU QUERIN, President JOE BOTTONI, Vice President AL GRANATA, Vice-President ALBO OLIVI, Secretary, Treasurer GINO DALLEVEDOVE, Plumber RINO BOTTONI, Plumber KYLE RUNCH, Plumber FRANCESCO COLAGIACOMO, Plumber ALEXANDER BOTTONI, Plumber DANIEL OLIVI, Plumber ALCESTE MERCATELLI, Plumber UMBERTO MERCATELLI, Plumber TONY LI, Plumber MIKE SMITH, Plumber ROSARIO FAZIO, Plumber ADAM SIST, Plumber JASON BUBNIC, Plumber ANTHONY SEMINAROTI, Plumber NICHOLAS NOVIA, Plumber DINO DELGESSO, Plumber NICK DEMARIA, Plumber MICHAEL ACURI, Plumber CARLO GUIDA, Plumber CLARA BOZZO, Account Manager

COSIMO LENTILE, Welder, Shop Laborer
FRANK GAROFALO, Welder, Shop Laborer
DARREN CABRAL, Sprinkler Fitter
ANTHONY DE ROSE, Sprinkler Fitter
LEO TORRES, Sprinkler Fitter

Ontario Cutting and Coring	STEVE LAKI GARY OSHUST CORY LONG MARK ZAPPAROLI LEO CHEVREFILS
Pengelly Iron Works	HUGH BALKOWSKI, Vice President JOSEPH PETRILLO XIAO BING JING EDWARD BALKOWSKI MINK KWAN
Priestly Demolition Inc.	VIC PRIESTLY, Owner RYAN PRIESTLY, President JONATHAN ZUBER, Safety Manager CARMELO PASTORE, Superintendent BRIAN PRIESTLY, Foreman MARK STICKWOOD, Operator R.J RAYMOND, Operator GREG CUTIA, Laborer
Rochester Insulated Glass	RICK WOLK
Royal X	NATALE PANETTA
Sattler Stained Glass Studio	NORBERT SATTLER
SD Shading	JURGEN BORCHERT, Owner CHRIS BORCHERT, Owner JAY THATCHER, Installation
Semple Gooder Roofing Ltd.	PETER MCGOEY, Production Manager ALEX NELSON, Office Estimator PETER SJOUWERMAN, Sheetmetal MICHAEL MCGOEY, Sheetmetal RON NOSEWORTHY, Sheetmetal MANUEL PEREIRA, Roofer DOMINGOS ALMEDIA, Roofer PAULINO DA SILVA, Roofer MANUEL VEIRIA, Roofer JORGE FERREIRA, Roofer MANUEL FERREIRA, Roofer EDWARDO MENDES, Roofer FERNANDO ARCILA, Roofer SECUNDINO RINHEIRO, Roofer
Serious Stainless Inc.	MIKE KRIEGER VALENTINO DI DOMENICO SHANE LEAVER
Skyline Tree Service	RICHARD GLIMOUR, Owner SHAWN VANDERYAGT LUC LAMARCHE DAN BURTON
Slimlite Skylights Ontario Inc.	RON LEUNG
Soundtrap Noise Reduction	ROGER FOULDS NICK FOULDS
Synergy Systems Inc.	ROBERT CAMPOL, System Designer, General Manager CHAD TRUDE, Project Manager JEFF LOCKYEAR, Senior Programmer DAVE FAST, Senior Field Technician TONY TRUDE, Junior Field Technician
Todd Pools Ltd.	DOUG TODD BRIAN TODD PATRICK DUNCALFE ROB SIBB JASON HOWELL
Topkote	JOE DECIANTIS, Owner EVAN MCPHERSON, Painter JOSE CUBIAS, Assistant

Total Pool and Spa Limited	LORNE ROSEN, Owner and Project Manager CHRIS AKELAITIS MARK AKELAITIS AUSTIN ARMSTRONG PAUL ARMSTRONG JUSTIN CORDIOVANI MICHAEL DOMINSKI BLAKE FLEISCHACKER MELISSA FLEISCHACKER JEOFFREY JOSE WARREN LEVINE BRENT LOUDON GERRY MCDONALD DURAN RENAULD JOHN SCANNELL
Tremonte Manufacturing Limited	SAM MONTELEONE, Owner and Project Manager FELIX KRUTSKO, Welder DENNIS CHEVERS, Welder JOHNN AXEEZO, Assistant Welder OLEG KRAMER, Assistant Welder CARLO NARDUCCI, Deliveries IHOR, Assistant Welder ADRIANO, Assistant Welder
Two Degrees North	SIMON COOPER, Owner and Project Manager JESSE CHAMPAGNE CONNIE CHISHOLM ANDREW WALLER SIMON WING
TWP Incorporated	MARCEL MULDER, Owner KAREN BUGGY, Office KAREN MULDER, Office ISRAEL GEORGE, Shop WILFRED PARSONS, Shop RICHARD PARSONS, Shop VINCENT GEORGE, Shop NOAH ODURO, Shop CARLOS PIRES, Shop PETER KUO, Shop RAYMOND SAMAROO, Shop REN KUO, Shop NORMAN LOVE, Shop WING CHAN, Shop GEORGE CHUNG, Shop IAN LEACH, Design Details
Upper Canada Specialty Hardware Ltd.	MIKE ORMOND
Wallis Inc.	GLEN WALLIS, Owner IAN MCRONALD VATHANA EAN
Best Boys	SAM & SIMON

An exhibition documenting the design and construction of the Integral House was specially prepared and shown in the Dyett Gallery at the School of Architecture and Planning at the University at Buffalo in spring 2006 to coincide with Brigitte Shim's Martell Lecture. The exhibition was designed by Shim·Sutcliffe and built in collaboration with students to explain the process of design development in architecture traced through a single project. It was planned around a series of work areas created within the gallery and brought together complete sets of drawings that included files of development sketches, notes and final contract documentation for numerous elements within the house.
In addition, the exhibition included a wide range of models of furniture and fireplaces, handrails and fittings, mock-ups and several full scale prototypes of building elements including door handles, balustrade assemblies and glazing systems. The exhibition provided an invaluable focus for student groups, tutorials and investigations into materials, design and fabrication.

Brigitte Shim was born in Kingston, Jamaica in 1958. Educated at the University of Waterloo in Canada, she received degrees in Environmental Studies and Architecture. Brigitte worked in Vancouver with Arthur Erickson and Associates and in Toronto with Baird/Sampson Architects.

A member of the University of Toronto's Faculty of Architecture, Landscape and Design since 1988, she teaches architecture design studios at both undergraduate and graduate levels and lectures on the history and theory of landscape architecture. She has been an Invited Visiting Professor at Harvard University's Graduate School of Design; Saarinen Visiting Professor, Bishop Visiting Professor and the Visiting Bicentennial Professor of Canadian Studies at Yale University's School of Architecture; and Visiting Professor at the Ecole Polytechnique Federal de Lausanne in Switzerland.

Howard Sutcliffe was born in Yorkshire, England in 1958. A graduate of the University of Waterloo in Canada, he holds degrees in Environmental Studies and Architecture. Prior to opening the Shim·Sutcliffe studio in 1987, he worked with Paul Merrick and Barton Myers, and played a key role on several award winning competition teams including the Kitchener City Hall designed by KPMB Architects. He was the first recipient of Canada's Council for the Arts Ronald J. Thom Award for Early Design Achievement.

The work of Shim·Sutcliffe has been published internationally and honored with numerous awards, including the Toronto Arts Award for Architecture and Design in 2002, and eight Royal Architectural Institute of Canada Governor General's Medals and Awards for Architecture.

Christopher Martell completed the undergraduate program in architecture at the University at Buffalo, The State University of New York in 1996 and was awarded his M.Arch degree there in 2001. After working in practice he went on to develop his interest in lighting and theater. Moving to New York City, Chris worked as a lighting designer with Frost Lighting, Inc. on a range of theatrical productions, concerts and special events before setting up Key Lighting & Visual LLC, a lighting and production company that is the most technically advanced on the east coast. In 2004, Chris and his wife Sally generously agreed to support the Martell Distinguished Visiting Critic Program.

Chris talks enthusiastically about his education and experiences at the School of Architecture & Planning in Buffalo and of the significant benefits that the program provided him. Subsequently, he has found those benefits invaluable in developing his own professional career, and they have prompted a lifelong interest in design. Chris and Sally speak passionately about how they enjoy supporting the school in ways that help as many students as possible.

Acknowledgments

First and foremost, the generosity and enthusiasm of Christopher and Sally Martell have made this project possible.

A grant from the Graham Foundation for Advanced Studies in the Fine Arts awarded to help establish buffaloBOOKS – a series of publications originating from the School of Architecture and Planning at UB – has been important to the realization of this project. The Foundation, and in particular the former Director Richard Solomon and Stephanie Whitlock, Director of Special Programs, have been committed supporters.

We are grateful to Brigitte Shim for the inspiration, ideas and genuine spirit of collaboration that she brought to our students and the architecture program in Buffalo. She dedicated considerable energy and time to the graduate design studio during the 2006 Spring Semester and gave an inspiring Martell Lecture to a packed auditorium on March 31. In addition, Brigitte and her partner Howard Sutcliffe, together with colleagues in their studio, designed an exhibition of their work that was first shown in the Dyett Gallery at UB. The Integral House exhibition was made possible with the support of the Dean's Office at the School of Architecture and Planning and the Canadian-American Studies Program at the University at Buffalo, The State University of New York. Special thanks are due to Dr. Lorraine Oak, the Director of that program.

The drawings and photographs of projects in this book have been published with the assistance of Shim·Sutcliffe. Thanks are due to the staff working in that studio, in particular Betsy Williamson. Mike Goorevich, assisted by Andrew Hart, played a leading role in the preparation of the exhibition.

Photographer Ed Burtynsky created a unique record of the preparation of the site and subsequent construction of the Integral House and has generously allowed those images to be included in this book.

Professor Mehrdad Hadighi, the chair of architecture at UB, has given his wholehearted support and invaluable assistance to the planning and realization of this program. Brigitte Shim's visits to the school were arranged by the staff in the Dean's Office. The 2006 Martell Lecture was recorded with the help of Maryanne Schultz, the curator of the School's Visual Resource Center, and Ryan Finley, a graduate student in the Architecture Program at UB. This publication has been designed by Christian Unverzagt and his colleague Neil Meredith at M1 in Detroit. Their creative insights and patience have been central to transforming a lecture into the book in your hand.

Illustration Credits

Edward Burtynsky: 11, 57-67
James Dow: 12a, 13, 14, 16, 17a, 17c, 18b, 19, 29
Steven Evans: 18a
Bob Gundu: 34, 39
Mark Heitoff: 71
Raimund Koch: 12b, 15

Drawing on page 27 courtesy of Mariani Metals.

All other images courtesy Shim·Sutcliffe Architects.

Integral House project credi current through Fall 2006.